101 best campsi

by the **beach**

2015

Compiled by: **Alan Rogers Travel Ltd**

Designed by: **Vine Design Ltd**

© Alan Rogers Travel Ltd 2014

Published by: **Alan Rogers Travel Ltd,**
Spelmonden Old Oast, Goudhurst, Kent TN17 1HE
Tel: 01580 214000 www.alanrogers.com

British Library Cataloguing-in-Publication Data:
A catalogue record for this book is
available from the British Library.

ISBN 978-1-909057-57-9

Printed in Great Britain by
Stephens & George Print Group

Contents

Welcome to the Alan Rogers
'101' guides

The Alan Rogers guides have been helping campers and caravanners make informed decisions about their holiday destinations since 1968. Today, whether online or in print, Alan Rogers still provides an independent, impartial view, with detailed reports, on each campsite.

With so much unfiltered, unqualified information freely available, the Alan Rogers perspective is invaluable to make sure you make the right choice for your holiday.

What is the '101' series?

At Alan Rogers, we know that readers have many and diverse interests, hobbies and particular requirements. And we know that our guides, featuring a total of some 3,000 campsites, can provide a bewildering choice from which it can be difficult to produce a shortlist of possible holiday destinations.

The Alan Rogers 101 guides are devised as a means of presenting a realistic, digestible number of great campsites, featured because of their suitability to a given theme.

This book remains first and foremost an authoritative guide to excellent campsites which offer great seaside holidays.

101 Best campsites
by the beach

For many, a holiday is not a holiday unless a beach is involved. And none more so than camping holidays. The archetypal sun, sea and sand holiday is, for some, the ideal; for others it's dramatic blustery seascapes and clattering, pebble beaches; yet others prefer secluded little coves and rocky inlets.

Whichever you prefer, this guide features campsites that offer all kinds of beach. There are even wonderful campsites set beside magnificent lakes, complete with their own beach.

So whether you're planning an out-of-season, invigorating seaside break or the full, sandy, bucket and spade extravaganza this summer, read on. There are 101 campsites in this guide and, depending on what kind of beach you're looking for, you are sure to find your ideal holiday destination here.

Alan Rogers – in search
of 'the best'

Alan Rogers himself started off with the very specific aim of providing people with the necessary information to allow them to make an informed decision about their holiday destination. Today we still do that with a range of guides that now covers Europe's best campsites in 27 countries. We work with campsites all day, every day. We visit campsites for inspection purposes (or even just for pleasure!). We know campsites 'inside out'.

We know which campsites would suit active families; which are great for get-away-from-it-all couples; we know which campsites are planning super new pool complexes; which campsites offer a fantastic menu in their on-site restaurant; which campsites allow you to launch a small boat from their slipway; which campsites have a decent playing area for kicking a ball around; which campsites have flat, grassy pitches and which have solid hard standings.

All Alan Rogers guides (and our website) are respected for their independent, impartial and honest assessment. The reviews are prose-based, without overuse of indecipherable icons and symbols. Our simple aim is to help guide you to a campsite that best matches your requirements – often quite difficult in today's age of information overload.

What is
the best?

The criteria we use when inspecting and selecting sites are numerous, but the most important by far is the question of good quality. People want different things from their choice of campsite, so campsite 'styles' vary dramatically: from small peaceful campsites in the heart of the countryside, to 'all singing, all dancing' sites in popular seaside resorts.

The size of the site, whether it's part of a chain or privately owned, makes no difference in terms of it being required to meet our exacting standards in respect of its quality and it being 'fit for purpose'. In other words, irrespective of the size of the site, or the number of facilities it offers, we consider and evaluate the welcome, the pitches, the sanitary facilities, the cleanliness, the general maintenance and even the location.

Expert
opinions

We rely on our dedicated team of Site Assessors, all of whom are experienced campers, caravanners or motorcaravanners, to visit and recommend campsites. Each year they travel around Europe inspecting new campsites for Alan Rogers and re-inspecting the existing ones.

When planning
your holiday...

A holiday should always be a relaxing affair, and a campsite-based holiday particularly so. Our aim is for you to find the ideal campsite for your holiday, one that suits your requirements. All Alan Rogers guides provide a wealth of information, including some details supplied by campsite owners themselves, and the following points may help ensure that you plan a successful holiday.

Find out more

An Alan Rogers reference number (eg FR12345) is given for each campsite and can be useful for finding more information and pictures online at www.alanrogers.com. Simply enter this number in the 'Campsite Search' field on the Home page.

Campsite descriptions

We aim to convey an idea of its general appearance, 'feel' and features, with details of pitch numbers, electricity, hardstandings etc.

Facilities

We list specific information on the site's facilities and amenities and, where available, the dates when these facilities are open (if not for the whole season). Much of this information is as supplied to us and may be subject to change. Should any particular activity or aspect of the campsite be important to you, it is always worth discussing with the campsite before you travel.

Swimming pools

Opening dates, any charges and levels of supervision are provided where we have been notified. In some countries (notably France) there is a regulation whereby Bermuda-style shorts may not be worn in swimming pools (for health and hygiene reasons). It is worth ensuring that you do take 'proper' swimming trunks with you.

Charges

Those given are the latest provided to us, usually 2014 prices, and should be viewed as a guide only.

Toilet blocks

Unless we comment otherwise, toilet blocks will be equipped with a reasonable number of British style WCs, washbasins and hot showers in cubicles. We also assume that there will be an identified chemical toilet disposal point, and that the campsite will provide water and waste water drainage points and bin areas. If not the case, we comment. We do mention certain features that some readers find important: washbasins in cubicles, facilities for babies, facilities for those with disabilities and motorcaravan service points.

Reservations

Necessary for high season (roughly mid-July to mid-August) in popular holiday areas (i.e. beach resorts). You can reserve many sites via our own Alan Rogers Travel Service or through other tour operators. Remember, many sites are closed all winter and you may struggle to get an answer.

Telephone numbers

All numbers assume that you are phoning from within the country in question. From the UK or Ireland, dial 00, then the country's prefix (e.g. France is 33), then the campsite number given, but dropping the first '0'.

Opening dates

Dates given are those provided to us and can alter before the start of the season. If you intend to visit shortly after a published opening date, or shortly before the closing date, it is wise to check that it will actually be open at the time required. Similarly some sites operate a restricted service during the low season, only opening some of their facilities (e.g. swimming pools) during the main season; where we know about this, and have the relevant dates, we indicate it – again if you are at all doubtful it is wise to check.

Accommodation

Over recent years, more and more campsites have added high quality mobile homes, chalets, lodges, gîtes and more. Where applicable we indicate what is available and you'll find details online.

Special Offers

Some campsites have taken the opportunity to highlight a special offer. This is arranged by them and for clarification please contact the campsite direct.

Life's
a beach

The lure of the coast, and the beach in particular, is a strong holiday motivation. Most people enjoy a holiday beside the sea and the many facets a beach has to offer holidaymakers of all ages. There are thousands of campsites across Europe, with many on or close to a great beach either on the coast or beside a shimmering lake. This guide features a shortlist of just 101, so read on and start dreaming…

Why
the beach...?

In the UK, it was not until the advent of the train in the late 19th century that the masses began to enjoy the benefits of a seaside holiday, fuelling the growth of long piers. Later, from the 1920s, glamour became part of the mix, with the south of France attracting the likes of Hemingway and Picasso. An hotel was encouraged to stay open all summer and the Côte d'Azur has never looked back. Venerable fashionable resorts (Biarritz, La Baule) are still going strong; sandy expanses in the West Country are perennial favourites; the blustery Scandanavian beaches are atmospheric and unspoilt; and the vast sandy beaches of the Spanish Costas offer a special magic.

Finding the right
beach campsite

Sun, sea and sand...it sounds simple but finding the right balance can be difficult with a campsite beach holiday. Some people want to be right there in the action, right on the beach; others prefer a campsite that's set back from the hurly-burly, even if it means a short drive. Some simply want miles of sand, with or without the crowds, others search for secluded rocky coves, perhaps seeking out that perfect spot beneath a shady pine.

You will find campsites with majestic sweeping sea views, campsites which run regular shuttle buses to and from the beach – especially handy when parking is at a premium; some campsites have their very own private stretch of beach and this may vary between sand, shingle, craggy rocks and dunes.

Quality Beaches

What makes a good beach? Which is the best beach in the area? Which beach is best for children? These are all valid questions but everyone will have their own opinion.

Blue Flag

Blue Flag is a prestigious international award scheme for beaches which acts as a guarantee of quality. Awarded annually to over 3,450 beaches and marinas in 41 countries, the award of a Blue Flag is based on compliance with 32 criteria covering the aspects of environmental education and information, water quality, environmental management, safety and services.

Children
on beaches

Family memories are made of long sunny days at the beach: splashing in the shallows, sandcastles, sandy sandwiches, buckets of crabs.

A good family beach, especially for young children, will have clean sand (ideally of the kind that makes good sandcastles), gently sloping down to the sea. Hopefully the sea at low tide is not a mile away, allowing toddlers to paddle while remaining close by (although a lovely wide beach does allow plenty of room for games and kite flying). And of course an ice cream vendor can usually bring a few squeals of pleasure!

Activities
for children

Some larger beaches often have activities specially for children, usually in high season – these could range from playgrounds or boating lakes right up to paid-for clubs with organised activities all day. And of course, in the UK the traditional donkey ride still exists!

For the younger ones

- Dig a channel to the sea

- Make a dam

- Bury dad in the sand

- Go beach combing for the most interesting "find"

- Build a boat or a car in the sand big enough to sit in – always makes an amusing snap for the album!

Ping Pong Ball Race

Dig a series of sloping channels wide enough (and smooth enough) to take a ping pong ball. Place ping pong balls at the start line and then race each other, blowing the ball down the channel to the finish line.

Beach Minigolf

Create your own minigolf course in the sand. Players take turns with a plastic golf club and ball – or whatever implement you can find.

Frisbee

A perennial favourite. Set up some targets in the sand and see who can get closest, or arrange plastic bottles in the sand and try to knock them over.

Go prepared and keep a bat and ball in the car – there's always a demand for French cricket, boules, badminton and kite flying.

Water Fun

Many lakeside campsites, especially in Austria, Hungary and Slovenia, have pedaloes, rowing boats and floating pontoons, as well as on-shore activities.

Activities
on the beach

With a bracing breeze, a good boost of ozone and loads of space, a beach always seems to invite activity.

It could be a fairly sedate activity like beach combing, throwing the odd stick for the dog or flying a kite.

Fishing too is popular, available all year, and for free.

More strenuous and physical activities might include power kiting and sand yachting

– popular on the long, wide, flat sandy beaches.

Surfing

By definition, good surfing beaches will involve turbulent waters so try and surf where a lifeguard is present and not on your own. Only surf within your own ability and experience, making sure you are surfing in safe locations.

Kayaking

A great way to spend time on the water but don't take this too lightly – you should be familiar with the necessary kit and precautions. Check the weather, wind and tides, wear a buoyancy aid and ideally paddle in a group, telling someone back on land where you are going. Make sure you can get back on board your kayak should you capsize.

Staying safe
at the beach

Beaches are a fun environment but it pays to be aware of potential dangers. In particular, keep an eye on tides – incoming tides can quickly trap people in coves or under cliffs. If unsure, check with a lifeguard. The RNLI beach safety tips are applicable anywhere.

Top Tips

- Always swim at a lifeguarded beach
- Swim between the red and yellow flags *(UK)*
- Never swim alone
- Never use inflatables in strong winds or rough seas
- If you get into trouble, wave and call for help
- If you see someone else in trouble, tell a lifeguard or call emergency services
- Take note of warnings and notices

Enjoy...!

Whether you're an 'old hand' or are contemplating your first trip, a regular reader of our Guides or a new 'convert', we wish you well in your travels and hope we have been able to help in some way. We are, of course, also out and about ourselves, visiting sites, talking to owners and readers, and generally checking on standards and new developments. We hope to bump into you!

Wishing you thoroughly enjoyable camping and caravanning in 2015 – favoured by good weather of course!

The Alan Rogers Team

Further
information

www.goodbeachguide.co.uk – *Website of the Marine Conservation Society*

www.blueflag.org – *The international organisation responsible for awarding the Blue Flag for beaches (and marinas)*

www.onbeach.nl – *Dutch website with information and lists of European beaches*

www.maplage.fr – *French website with extensive information on French beaches*

www.esplaya.com – *English-language website on the many beaches in Spain*

www.italyheaven.co.uk – *English-language website on the beaches of Italy*

www.kustgids.nl and www.holland.com – *Respectively, a Dutch and an English-language website on the beaches of the Netherlands*

Kompas Camping Nieuwpoort

Brugsesteenweg 49, B-8620 Nieuwpoort (West Flanders)
t: 058 236 037   e: nieuwpoort@kompascamping.be
alanrogers.com/BE0550   www.kompascamping.be

Accommodation: ☑ Pitch   ☑ Mobile home/chalet   ○ Hotel/B&B   ○ Apartment

Not far from Dunkerque and Calais and convenient for the A18 motorway, this large, well equipped and well run site with 1056 pitches caters particularly for families. There are many amenities including a heated pool complex, a range of sporting activities, play areas and a children's farm. The 469 touring pitches, all with 10A electricity, are in regular rows on flat grass in various parts of the site; 120 also have a water point and waste water drainage. With many seasonal units and caravan holiday homes, the site becomes full during Belgian holidays and in July and August. A network of footpaths links all areas of the site. Gates to the rear lead to a reservoir reserved for sailing, windsurfing and canoeing (canoes for hire) during certain hours only. Although the site is vast, there is a sense of spaciousness thanks to the broad stretch of landscaped leisure areas. The site is well fenced with a card-operated barrier and a night guard. The whole area is a paradise for cyclists with access to over 200 km. of cycle-friendly paths and roads.

Facilities: Five modern, clean and well maintained toilet blocks include washbasins in cubicles, controllable showers and excellent facilities for families, young children and disabled visitors. Dishwashing and laundry rooms. Washing machines and dryers. Motorcaravan services. Supermarket, bakery, restaurant, takeaway and café/bar (all w/ends low season, otherwise daily). Swimming pools (heated and supervised) with slide, paddling pool and pool games (17/5-14/9). Bicycle hire. Tennis. Extensive adventure playgrounds. Multisports court. Entertainment programme in July/Aug. WiFi throughout (charged). Off site: Fishing within 500 m. Nearest village 2 km. Riding 3 km. Beach 4 km. Golf driving range 5 km.

Open: 28 March - 12 November.

Directions: From Dunkerque on A18 (E40) take exit 3. At roundabout take fourth exit (small road, easily missed). At junction turn left on N356. At end of this road at T-junction, turn right on N367. Site is on the left in 300 m.

GPS: 51.12965, 2.77222

Charges guide

Per unit incl. 4 persons and electricity	€ 25,90 - € 39,90
dog	€ 2,90

Largest unit accepted 2.5x8 m.

You might like to know

Bicycles can be hired on the campsite and are a fun way to explore the seafront!

○ Beach on site
○ Beach within 1 km
☑ Sandy beach
○ Blue Flag quality
○ Lifeguard *(high season)*
○ Sun lounger and/or deckchair hire
☑ Watersports *(e.g. sailing or windsurfing)*
○ Snacks and drinks
○ Sunshades/sunbeds
☑ Dogs allowed *(on the beach)*

Camping Ter Duinen

Wenduinsesteenweg 143, B-8420 De Haan (West Flanders)
t: 050 413 593 e: info@campingterduinen.be
alanrogers.com/BE0578 www.campingterduinen.be

Accommodation: ☑ Pitch ☑ Mobile home/chalet ○ Hotel/B&B ○ Apartment

Ter Duinen is a large, seaside holiday site with 120 touring pitches and over 700 privately owned static holiday caravans. The pitches are laid out in straight lines with tarmac access roads and the site has three immaculate toilet blocks. Other than a bar and a playing field, the site has little else to offer, but it is only a 600 m. walk to the sea and next door to the site is a large sports complex with a sub-tropical pool and several sporting facilities. Opportunities for riding and golf (18-hole course) are close by. It is possible to hire bicycles in the town. Access to the beach is via a good woodland footpath. There is a main road and tramway to cross, but there are designated pedestrian crossings. Cycling is very popular in this area and there are numerous good cycle paths, including one into the centre of De Haan (1.5 km). The best places to visit for a day trip are Ostend with the Atlantic Wall from WWII, Knokke (which holds many summer festivals) and Bruges.

You might like to know

The campsite is ideally situated for day trips to Bruges, Knokke and Ostend.

○ Beach on site
☑ Beach within 1 km
☑ Sandy beach
○ Blue Flag quality
○ Lifeguard *(high season)*
○ Sun lounger and/or deckchair hire
○ Watersports *(e.g. sailing or windsurfing)*
○ Snacks and drinks
○ Sunshades/sunbeds
○ Dogs allowed *(on the beach)*

Facilities: Three modern toilet blocks have good fittings, washbasins in cubicles (hot and cold water) and showers (€ 1.20). Baby bath. Facilities for disabled visitors. Laundry facilities with two washing machines and a dryer, irons and ironing boards. Motorcaravan services. Shop. Snack bar and takeaway. Internet room (charged). Off site: Bicycle hire and sea with sandy beach 600 m. Riding 1 km. Golf 3 km. Boat launching 6 km. A bus for Bruges stops 200 m. from the site, a tram for the coast 400 m.

Open: 15 March - 15 October.

Directions: On E40/A10 in either direction take exit 6 for De Haan/Jabbeke. Follow N377 towards Haan-Bredene, at roundabout head towards Vlissegem. After 4 km. go straight on at junction. Turn right after a further 1.5 km. Site is 750 m. on right.

GPS: 51.28318, 3.05753

Charges guide

Per unit incl. 4 persons and electricity	€ 19,00 - € 28,00
extra person	€ 3,50
child (under 10 yrs)	€ 3,00
dog	€ 3,50

Facilities: The six toilet blocks (three heated) are of exemplary quality. Washing machines and dryers. Motorcaravan services. Gas supplies. Supermarket, restaurant, bar and takeaway (all season). Snack kiosk at beach. Lifeguards on duty. Tennis. Minigolf. Bicycle hire. Canoe and pedalo hire. Boat launching. Playgrounds. Doctor calls. Dogs are not accepted. New chalet for disabled visitors. Camping accessories shop. Car hire. Car wash. WiFi (charged).
Off site: Fishing 500 m. Water-skiing and windsurfing 1 km. Riding 5 km. Golf 8 km. Boatyard with maintenance facilities.

Open: 27 March - 31 October.

Directions: On the Bellinzona-Locarno road 13, exit Tenero. Site is signed at Co-op roundabout. Coming from the south, enter Tenero and follow signs to site.

GPS: 46.16895, 8.85592

Charges guide

Per unit incl. 2 persons
and electricity CHF 39,00 - CHF 90,00

extra person CHF 9,00 - CHF 11,00

Some pitches have min. stay regulations. Discounts for stays over 10 days and for seniors.

Switzerland – Tenero

Camping Campofelice

Via alle Brere 7, CH-6598 Tenero (Ticino)
t: 091 745 1417   e: camping@campofelice.ch
alanrogers.com/CH9890   www.campofelice.ch

Accommodation: ☑ Pitch   ○ Mobile home/chalet   ○ Hotel/B&B   ○ Apartment

Considered by many to be the best family campsite in Switzerland, Campofelice is bordered on the front by Lake Maggiore and on one side by the Verzasca estuary, where the site has its own marina. It is divided into rows, with 721 generously sized touring pitches on flat grass on either side of hard access roads. Mostly well shaded, all pitches have electricity connections (10-13A, 360 Europlug) and 410 also have water, drainage and TV connections. Pitches near the lake cost more (these are not available for motorcaravans until September) and a special area is reserved for small tents. A little more expensive than other sites in the area, but excellent value for the range and quality of the facilities. Sporting facilities are good and there are cycle paths in the area, including into Locarno. A free shuttle bus runs to Locarno ferry terminal. The beach by the lake is sandy, long and wider than the usual lakeside ones, and has now been extended, with well kept lawns for sunbathing. It shelves gently so that bathing is safe for children.

You might like to know

The site lies on the sandy shores of Lake Maggiore, where there is safe swimming and a private beach. Kayaks and canoes are available to hire from the site's own harbour.

- ☑ Beach on site
- ○ Beach within 1 km
- ☑ Sandy beach
- ○ Blue Flag quality
- ☑ Lifeguard *(high season)*
- ○ Sun lounger and/or deckchair hire
- ☑ Watersports *(e.g. sailing or windsurfing)*
- ☑ Snacks and drinks
- ○ Sunshades/sunbeds
- ○ Dogs allowed *(on the beach)*

Camping Lanterna

Lanterna 1, Tar-Vabriga, HR-52465 Porec (Istria)
t: 052 465 010   e: camping@valamar.com
alanrogers.com/CR6716 www.camping-adriatic.com

Accommodation: ☑ Pitch   ☑ Mobile home/chalet   ○ Hotel/B&B   ○ Apartment

This is a well organised site and one of the largest in Croatia with high standards and an amazing selection of activities, and is part of the Camping on the Adriatic group. Set in 80 hectares with over 3 km. of beach, there are 2,851 pitches, of which 1,887 are for touring units. All have 10A electricity and fresh water, and 225 also have waste water drainage. Pitches are 80-120 sq.m. with some superb locations right on the sea, although these tend to be taken first so it is advisable to book ahead. Some of the better pitches are in a reserved booking area. There are wonderful coastal views from some of the well shaded terraced pitches. Facilities at Lanterna are impressive with the whole operation running smoothly for the campers. The land is sloping in parts and terraced in others. There is a pool complex, including a large pool for children, in addition to the pretty bay with its rocky beaches and buoyed safety areas. A member of Leading Campings group.

You might like to know

A vast array of sports and watersports is available, both at the campsite and at the nearby Valeta Sport Centre.

☑ Beach on site
○ Beach within 1 km
○ Sandy beach
☑ Blue Flag quality
○ Lifeguard *(high season)*
○ Sun lounger and/or deckchair hire
☑ Watersports *(e.g. sailing or windsurfing)*
○ Snacks and drinks
☑ Sunshades/sunbeds
☑ Dogs allowed *(on the beach)*

Facilities: The sixteen sanitary blocks are clean and good quality. Facilities for children and baby care areas, some Turkish style WCs, hot showers, with some blocks providing facilities for disabled visitors. Three supermarkets sell most everyday requirements. Fresh fish shop. Four restaurants, bars and snack bars and fast food outlets. Swimming pool and two paddling pools. Sandpit and play areas, with entertainment for all in high season. Tennis. Bicycle hire. Watersports. Boat hire. Minigolf. Riding. Internet café. Jetty and ramp for boats. WiFi (free). Mobile homes for rent (Istria Prestige). Dogs are accepted in certain areas. Off site: Hourly bus service from the reception area. Fishing. Riding 500 m. Golf 2 km. Nearest supermarket in Novigrad 9 km.

Open: 1 April - 10 October.

Directions: The turn to Lanterna is well signed off the Novigrad to Porec road 8 km. south of Novigrad. Continue for 2 km. along the turn off road towards the coast and the campsite is on the right hand side.

GPS: 45.29672, 13.59442

Charges guide

Per unit incl. 2 persons and electricity	€ 16,90 - € 31,00
with full services	€ 18,30 - € 32,60
extra person	€ 4,40 - € 7,90
child (4-10 yrs)	no charge - € 5,40

Prices for pitches by the sea are higher.

Facilities: Fifteen toilet blocks of varying styles and ages provide toilets, open style washbasins and controllable hot showers. Child size toilets, washbasins and showers. Bathroom (free). Facilities for disabled visitors. Laundry with sinks and washing machines. Dog showers. Two supermarkets. Fish market (08.00-14.00). Souvenir shops and newspaper kiosk. Bars and restaurants with dance floor and stage (25/4-30/9). Pâtisserie. Tennis. Minigolf. Fishing (with permit). Bicycle hire. Games room. Marina with boat launching. Boat and pedalo hire. Disco outside entrance. Daily entertainment programme for children up to 12 yrs. Excursions organised. Two dedicated dog areas. WiFi. Off site: Riding 2 km.

Open: 19 April - 12 October.

Directions: Site is 2 km. north of Vrsar. Follow campsite signs from Vrsar.

GPS: 45.16522, 13.60723

Charges guide

Per unit incl. 2 persons and electricity € 17,50 - € 44,40	
extra person € 4,50 - € 9,20	
child (5-17 yrs) no charge - € 7,30	
dog € 2,50 - € 6,50	

Croatia – Vrsar

Camping Valkanela

Valkanela, HR-52450 Vrsar (Istria)
t: 052 445 216   e: valkanela@maistra.hr
alanrogers.com/CR6727   www.campingrovinjvrsar.com

Accommodation: ☑ Pitch   ○ Mobile home/chalet   ○ Hotel/B&B   ○ Apartment

Camping Valkanela is located in a beautiful green bay, right on the Adriatic Sea, between the villages of Vrsar and Funtana. It offers 1,300 pitches, all with 10A electricity. Pitches near the beach are numbered, have shade from mature trees and are slightly sloping towards the sea. Those towards the back of the site are on open fields without much shade and are not marked or numbered. Unfortunately, the number of pitches has increased dramatically over the years, many are occupied by seasonal campers and statics of every description, and these parts of the site are not very attractive. Most numbered pitches have water points close by, but the back pitches have to go to the toilet blocks for water. Access roads are gravel. For those who like activity, Valkanela has four gravel tennis courts, beach volleyball and opportunities for diving, water skiing and boat rental. There is a little marina for mooring small boats and a long rock and pebble private beach with some grass lawns for sunbathing. There may be some noise nuisance from the disco outside the entrance and during high season the site can become very crowded.

You might like to know

There are several beaches along the coastline between Vrsar and Funtana, including stone, pebble and sandy beaches.

- ☑ Beach on site
- ○ Beach within 1 km
- ○ Sandy beach
- ☑ Blue Flag quality
- ○ Lifeguard *(high season)*
- ☑ Sun lounger and/or deckchair hire
- ○ Watersports *(e.g. sailing or windsurfing)*
- ○ Snacks and drinks
- ○ Sunshades/sunbeds
- ☑ Dogs allowed *(on the beach)*

Facilities: Six modern and one refurbished toilet blocks with British style toilets, open washbasins and controllable hot showers. Child size facilities. Baby rooms. Family bathroom. Facilities for disabled visitors. Laundry service. Fridge box hire. Motorcaravan services. Shop. Three bars. Two restaurants. Large swimming pool. Playground. Fishing. Boat and pedalo hire. Miniclub (5-11 yrs). Excursions. Internet access in reception. WiFi (charged). Off site: Riding 2 km. Rovinj 5 km.

Open: 21 April - 1 October.

Directions: Site is on the coast 4 km. southeast of Rovinj. From Rovinj travel south towards Pula. After 4 km. turn right following campsite signs.

GPS: 45.05432, 13.68568

Charges guide

Per person € 5,00 - € 10,80	
child (5-18 yrs) no charge - € 9,20	
pitch incl. electricity € 7,00 - € 30,00	
dog € 3,10 - € 7,20	

Croatia – Rovinj

Camping Vestar

Vestar bb, HR-52210 Rovinj (Istria)
t: 052 803 700 e: vestar@maistra.hr
alanrogers.com/CR6733 www.campingrovinjvrsar.com

Accommodation: ☑ Pitch ☑ Mobile home/chalet ○ Hotel/B&B ○ Apartment

Camping Vestar is a quiet site just 5 km. from the historic harbour town of Rovinj, and is one of the rare sites in Croatia with a partly sandy beach. Right behind the beach is a large area, attractively landscaped with young trees and shrubs, with grass for sunbathing. The site has 650 large pitches, of which 500 are for touring units, all with 6/10A electricity (the rest being taken by seasonal units and 60 pitches for tour operators). It is largely wooded with good shade and from the bottom row of pitches there are views of the sea. Pitching is on two separate fields, one for free camping, the other with numbered pitches. Those at the beach are in a half circle around the shallow bay, making it safe for children to swim. Vestar has a small marina and a jetty for mooring small boats and excursions to the islands are arranged. There is a miniclub and live music with dancing at one of the bars/restaurants in the evenings. The restaurants all have open-air terraces, one covered with vines to protect you from the hot sun.

You might like to know

The beach (half pebble, half sand) is situated 5 km. from Rovinj.

☑ Beach on site
○ Beach within 1 km
☑ Sandy beach
☑ Blue Flag quality
○ Lifeguard *(high season)*
○ Sun lounger and/or deckchair hire
☑ Watersports *(e.g. sailing or windsurfing)*
○ Snacks and drinks
○ Sunshades/sunbeds
○ Dogs allowed *(on the beach)*

Facilities: Seven modern, well maintained toilet blocks (water heated by solar power) with open plan washbasins (some cabins for ladies) and free hot showers. Private family bathrooms for hire. Facilities for disabled visitors and children. Laundry sinks and washing machine. Motorcaravan services. Electric car/scooter charging point. Car wash. Mini-marina and boat crane. Supermarket. Bar. Restaurant and pizzeria (May-18/10). Playground. Daily children's club. Evening shows with live music. Boat launching. Fishing. Diving centre. Motorboat hire. WiFi (free). Airport transfers. Off site: Wellness and fitness centre 500 m. Historic town of Cres with bars, restaurants and shops 2 km. Coastal cycle path.

Open: 27 March - 18 October.

Directions: From Rijeka take the coast road E65 towards Senj and Split. After 20 km. follow signs for Krk island (reached over bridge). Continue on the 102 for 20 km. then the 104 to Valbiska-Merag ferry. From Merag drive to the town of Cres where, at the beginning of the town, site is signed to the right. There is a ferry from Brestova to Porozina but the road on to Cres is only suitable for smaller units.

GPS: 44.96346, 14.39747

Charges guide

Per unit incl. 2 persons and electricity	€ 18,20 - € 37,20
extra person	€ 6,20 - € 12,50
child (3-12 yrs)	€ 2,80 - € 5,20
dog	no charge - € 3,00

Croatia – Cres

Camping Kovacine

Melin I/20, HR-51557 Cres (Kvarner)
t: 051 573 150   e: campkovacine@kovacine.com
alanrogers.com/CR6765   www.camp-kovacine.com

Accommodation: ☑ Pitch ☑ Mobile home/chalet ○ Hotel/B&B ○ Apartment

Camping Kovacine is located on a peninsula on the beautiful Kvarner island of Cres, just 2 km. from the town of the same name. The site has just under 1000 pitches for touring units, most with 16A electricity (from renewable sources) and water supply. On sloping ground, partially shaded by mature olive and pine trees, pitching is on the large, open spaces between the trees. From the waterside pitches there are far reaching views over the sea to the coast beyond. Kovacine is partly an FKK (naturist) site, which is quite common in Croatia, and has a pleasant atmosphere. The site has its own beach (Blue Flag), part concrete, part pebbles, and a jetty for mooring boats and fishing. It is close to the historic town of Cres, the main town on the island, which offers a rich history of fishing, shipyards and authentic Kvarner-style houses. There are also several bars, restaurants and shops.

You might like to know

For stays of 10 consecutive days, site refunds the cost of a one way ferry journey to the island of Cres; or the cost of a return journey for 18 consecutive days.

☑ Beach on site
○ Beach within 1 km
○ Sandy beach
☑ Blue Flag quality
☑ Lifeguard *(high season)*
○ Sun lounger and/or deckchair hire
☑ Watersports *(e.g. sailing or windsurfing)*
☑ Snacks and drinks
○ Sunshades/sunbeds
☑ Dogs allowed *(on the beach)*

Croatia – Nin

Zaton Holiday Resort

Draznikova ulica 76 t, HR-23232 Nin (Dalmatia)
t: 023 280 215   e: camping@zaton.hr
alanrogers.com/CR6782   www.zaton.hr

Accommodation: ☑ Pitch   ☑ Mobile home/chalet   ○ Hotel/B&B   ☑ Apartment

Facilities: Five modern and one refurbished toilet blocks with washbasins (some in cabins) and controllable hot showers. Child-size washbasins. Family shower rooms. Facilities for disabled visitors. Outdoor grill station. Motorcaravan services. Car wash. Shopping centre. Restaurants (self-service one has breakfast, lunch and evening menus). Several bars and kiosks. Water play area for children. Outdoor swimming pools. Mini-car track. Riding. Tennis centre. Trim track. Scuba diving. Professional entertainment team. Teen club. Games hall. WiFi. New (2014) beach extension with climbing pyramids. Live shows on stage by the beach. Off site: Historic towns of Zadar (parking difficult) and Nin 3 km.

Open: 25 April - 30 September.

Directions: From Rijeka take no. 2 road south or A1/E65 Autobahn leave at exit for Zadar. Drive north towards Nin, Zaton Holiday Resort is signed a few kilometres before Nin.
GPS: 44.234767, 15.164367

Charges guide

Per unit incl. 2 persons and electricity	€ 23,70 - € 55,90
extra person	€ 6,00 - € 11,90
child (1-11 yrs acc. to age)	€ 3,30 - € 9,40
dog	€ 5,00 - € 9,90

Zaton Holiday Resort is a modern family holiday park with a one and a half kilometre private sandy beach. It is close to the historic town of Nin and just a few kilometres from the ancient city of Zadar. This park itself is more like a large village and has every amenity one can think of for a holiday on the Dalmatian coast. The village is divided into two areas separated by a public area with reception, bakery, shops, restaurant and a large car park, one for campers close to the sea, the other for a complex with holiday apartments. Zaton has 1,030 mostly level pitches for touring units, all with electricity, water and waste water. All numbered pitches have shade from mature trees and some have views over the extensive, 2 km long sandy beach and the sea. Access is off hard access roads. Zaton caters for everybody's needs on site with numerous bars, restaurants, shops and two swimming pools. Excursions are organised to the Krka waterfalls, the Zrmanja Canyon and the Kornati, Paklenica and Plitvice National Parks. A member of Leading Campings group.

You might like to know

Zaton Holiday Resort is in a breathtaking region, within a two-hour drive of four national parks and two nature parks. The historic town of Nin (2 km) is known for its medicinal mud (peloid).

☑ Beach on site
○ Beach within 1 km
☑ Sandy beach
☑ Blue Flag quality
☑ Lifeguard *(high season)*
☑ Sun lounger and/or deckchair hire
☑ Watersports *(e.g. sailing or windsurfing)*
☑ Snacks and drinks
☑ Sunshades/sunbeds
☑ Dogs allowed *(on the beach)*

Facilities: Two modern, attractive and well maintained sanitary blocks, one completely renovated in 2013, have a special children's area and a baby bath. Showers (on payment). Bathrooms to rent. Laundry room with washing machines and dryer. Shop (1/4-30/10). Bar. Restaurant. Takeaway. Indoor heated swimming pool. Sauna, massage and cosmetic studio. Bowling alley. Small zoo. Indoor playroom (free entry). Volleyball. Watersports centre with windsurfing, sailing and catamaran sailing. Go-kart and bicycle hire. WiFi over site and Internet in reception (charged). Off site: Riding 200 m. Golf 8 km. Schwerin Schloss, Wismar (can be reached by cycleway). Rostock and Lübeck.

Open: All year.

Directions: Site is on the coast 6 km. northwest of Wismar. Leave Autobahn 20 at exit 8 Wismar Mitte, north to Gägelow then north on minor road to Zierow.

GPS: 53.9347, 11.3718

Charges guide

Per unit incl. 2 persons and electricity	€ 20,30 - € 29,70
extra person	€ 4,50 - € 5,70
child (5-14 yrs)	no charge - € 3,00
dog	€ 3,00

Germany – Zierow

Ostsee-Camping

Strandstrasse 19c, D-23968 Zierow (Mecklenburg-West Pomerania)
t: 038 428 638 20 e: ostseecampingzierow@t-online.de
alanrogers.com/DE25000 www.ostsee-camping.de

Accommodation: ☑ Pitch ☑ Mobile home/chalet ○ Hotel/B&B ☑ Apartment

Set on top of sand dunes overlooking and with direct access to the beach, Ostsee Camping is in a quiet location yet within easy reach of major towns in the region. There is good swimming from the beach, although the site does have a small swimming pool. Of the 486 level pitches, 321 are for touring units, all have electricity connections (10-16A) and 120 are fully serviced. They are set on grass and in places there is some tree shade. Outside the site there are eight quickstop facilities with electricity connections. This is a good site for families, with entertainment programmes in summer, playgrounds and a gently shelving, sandy beach. This part of Germany, formally the DDR, is not that well known to tourists, yet it has a great deal to offer in the way of sandy beaches, attractive landscapes and historic towns, cities and buildings. Anyone travelling to the Baltic coast should allow a few hours to visit Schwerin with The Schloss and its gardens, set on an island in the Schweriner lake, the second largest in Northern Germany.

You might like to know

This all-year, family campsite is situated directly on the Baltic coast, between the old Hanseatic cities of Lübeck and Wismar.

☑ Beach on site
○ Beach within 1 km
☑ Sandy beach
○ Blue Flag quality
☑ Lifeguard *(high season)*
○ Sun lounger and/or deckchair hire
☑ Watersports *(e.g. sailing or windsurfing)*
☑ Snacks and drinks
○ Sunshades/sunbeds
☑ Dogs allowed *(on the beach)*

Germany – Wulfen

Camping Wulfener Hals

Wulfener Hals Weg 100, D-23769 Wulfen auf Fehmarn (Schleswig-Holstein)
t: 043 718 6280   e: info@wulfenerhals.de
alanrogers.com/DE30030   www.wulfenerhals.de

Accommodation: ☑ Pitch   ☑ Mobile home/chalet   ○ Hotel/B&B   ☑ Apartment

This is a top class, all year round site suitable as a stopover or as a base for a longer stay. Attractively situated by the sea, it is large, mature (34 hectares) and well maintained. It has over 800 individual pitches (half for touring) of up to 160 sq.m. in glades. Some are separated by bushes providing shade in the older parts, less so in the newer areas nearer the sea. There are many hardstandings and all pitches have electricity, water and drainage. Some new rental accommodation has been added, including a 'honeymoon mobile home'. A separate area has been developed for motorcaravans. It provides 60 extra large pitches, all with electricity, water and drainage, and some with TV aerial points, together with a new toilet block. There is much to do for young and old alike at Wulfener Hals, with a new heated outdoor pool and paddling pool (unsupervised), although the sea is naturally popular as well. The site also has many sporting facilities including its own golf courses and schools for watersports. A member of Leading Campings group.

You might like to know

This is a great location for watersports enthusiasts, with sailing, windsurfing and kitesurfing (courses and equipment hire available).

☑ Beach on site
○ Beach within 1 km
☑ Sandy beach
○ Blue Flag quality
○ Lifeguard *(high season)*
○ Sun lounger and/or deckchair hire
☑ Watersports *(e.g. sailing or windsurfing)*
○ Snacks and drinks
○ Sunshades/sunbeds
○ Dogs allowed *(on the beach)*

Facilities: Five heated sanitary buildings have first class facilities including showers and both open washbasins and private cabins. Family bathrooms for rent. Facilities for children and disabled campers. Beauty, wellness and cosmetic facilities (April-Oct). Laundry. Motorcaravan services. Shop, bar, restaurants and takeaway (April-Oct). Swimming pool (May-Oct). Sauna. Solarium. Jacuzzi. Sailing, catamaran, windsurfing and diving schools. Boat slipway. Golf courses (18 holes, par 72 and 9 holes, par 3). Riding. Fishing. Archery. Well organised and varied entertainment programmes for all ages. Bicycle hire. Catamaran hire. WiFi over part of site (charged). Off site: Naturist beach 500 m.

Open: All year.

Directions: From Hamburg take A1/E47 north towards Puttgarden, after crossing the bridge to Fehmarn first exit to the right to Avendorf. In Avendorf turn left and follow the signs for Wulfen and the site.
GPS: 54.40805, 11.17374

Charges guide

Per unit incl. 2 persons and electricity	€ 17,80 - € 43,50
extra person	€ 5,00 - € 9,30
child (2-12 yrs)	€ 2,60 - € 5,20
dog	€ 3,00 - € 7,50

Surcharges for larger pitches. Many discounts available and special family prices.

Germany – Fehmarn

Strandcamping Wallnau

Wallnau 1, D-23769 Fehmarn (Schleswig-Holstein)
t: 043 729 456 e: wallnau@strandcamping.de
alanrogers.com/DE30070 www.strandcamping.de

Accommodation: ☑ Pitch ☑ Mobile home/chalet ○ Hotel/B&B ○ Apartment

Facilities: Heated sanitary blocks provide free showers. Child size toilets and showers. Baby rooms. Facilities for disabled visitors. Laundry facilities. Motorcaravan services. Shop. Bar, restaurant and snack bar. Open-air stage and soundproofed disco. Wellness, solarium and sauna. Archery. Watersports. Minigolf. Bouncy castles. Internet café. Beach fishing. Riding. WiFi (charged). Off site: Boat launching 6 km. Golf 16 km.

Open: 1 April - 26 October.

Directions: After crossing the bridge follow road to Landkirchen and Petersdorf. From Petersdorf site is signed. It is 4 km. northwest of the town.

GPS: 54.48761, 11.0186

Charges guide

Per unit incl. 2 persons and electricity	€ 18,20 - € 36,90
child (under 17 yrs)	€ 2,00 - € 6,00
extra person	€ 4,10 - € 7,70

No credit cards.

With direct beach access and protected from the wind by a dyke, this family site is on Germany's second largest island (since 1963 joined to the Baltic sea coast by a bridge). This is a quiet location on the western part of Fehmarn Island in close proximity to a large bird sanctuary. Of the 800 pitches, 400 are for touring, all with electricity (6-16A) and on level grass areas arranged in alleys and separated by hedges. The island is low lying, ideal for leisurely walking and cycling, especially along the track that runs along the top of the dyke. The beach is a mixture of sand and pebbles, and in summer lifeguards are on duty. The southern part is a naturist area. For those with an ornithological interest, the bird sanctuary with over 80 species is worth visiting. Swimming, sailing and diving are possible in the sea and there is a windsurfing school. For those who prefer dry land there is pony riding for children and a riding school. During summer there are entertainment programmes for children and courses for adults; twice a week there are film shows.

You might like to know

The site boasts a specialist kite- and windsurfing school, its own dive centre and riding stables. Additionally, the site is located next to the Wallnau bird sanctuary.

- ☑ Beach on site
- ○ Beach within 1 km
- ○ Sandy beach
- ○ Blue Flag quality
- ☑ Lifeguard *(high season)*
- ○ Sun lounger and/or deckchair hire
- ☑ Watersports *(e.g. sailing or windsurfing)*
- ○ Snacks and drinks
- ○ Sunshades/sunbeds
- ○ Dogs allowed *(on the beach)*

Denmark – Blavand

Hvidbjerg Strand Camping

Hvidbjerg Strandvej 27, DK-6857 Blavand (Ribe)
t: 75 27 90 40 e: info@hvidbjerg.dk
alanrogers.com/DK2010 www.hvidbjerg.dk

Accommodation: ☑ Pitch ☑ Mobile home/chalet ○ Hotel/B&B ○ Apartment

A family owned TopCamp holiday site, Hvidbjerg Strand is on the west coast near Blåvands Huk, 43 km. from Esbjerg. It is a high quality, seaside site with a wide range of amenities including a large wellness facility. Most of the 570 pitches have electricity (6/10A) and the 130 'comfort' pitches also have water, drainage and satellite TV. To the rear of the site, 70 new, fully serviced pitches have been developed, some up to 250 sq.m. and 44 with private sanitary facilities. Most pitches are individual and divided by hedges, in rows on flat sandy grass, with areas also divided by small trees and hedges. On-site leisure facilities include an indoor suite of supervised playrooms designed for all ages, with Lego, computers, video games, TV, etc. and an impressive, tropical-style indoor pool complex. This includes stalactite caves and a 70 m. water chute, the 'black hole' with sounds and lights, plus water slides, spa baths, Turkish bath and a sauna. A Blue Flag beach and windsurfing school are adjacent to the site and the town offers a full activity programme during high season. A member of Leading Campings group.

You might like to know

The special conditions here are due to the reef known as Horns Reef, which stretches 40 km. into the North Sea creating a lagoon on its south side.

- ☑ Beach on site
- ○ Beach within 1 km
- ☑ Sandy beach
- ☑ Blue Flag quality
- ○ Lifeguard *(high season)*
- ○ Sun lounger and/or deckchair hire
- ☑ Watersports *(e.g. sailing or windsurfing)*
- ○ Snacks and drinks
- ○ Sunshades/sunbeds
- ○ Dogs allowed *(on the beach)*

Facilities: Five superb toilet units include washbasins, roomy showers, spa baths, suites for disabled visitors, family bathrooms, kitchens and laundry facilities. Bathroom for children decorated with dinosaurs and Disney characters, and racing car baby baths. Motorcaravan services. Supermarket. Café/restaurant. TV rooms. Pool complex, solarium and sauna. Wellness facility. Western-themed indoor play hall. Play areas. Supervised play rooms (09.00-16.00 daily). Barbecue areas. Minigolf. Riding (Western style). Fishing. Dog showers. ATM machine. Free WiFi. Off site: Legoland 70 km.

Open: 20 March - 18 October.

Directions: From Varde take roads 181/431 to Blåvand. Site is signed left on entering the town.
GPS: 55.54600, 8.13507

Charges guide

Per unit incl. 2 persons and electricity	€ 33,80 - € 61,80
extra person	€ 10,90
child (0-11 yrs)	€ 8,10
dog	€ 4,00

Denmark – Fjerritslev

Klim Strand Camping

Havvejen 167, Klim Strand, DK-9690 Fjerritslev (Nordjylland)
t: 98 22 53 40 e: ksc@klim-strand.dk
alanrogers.com/DK2170 www.klim-strand.dk

Accommodation: ☑ Pitch ☑ Mobile home/chalet ○ Hotel/B&B ○ Apartment

A large family holiday site right beside the sea, Klim Strand is a paradise for children. It is a privately owned TopCamp site with a full complement of quality facilities, including its own fire engine and trained staff. The site has 460 numbered touring pitches, all with electricity (10A), laid out in rows, many divided by trees and hedges, with shade in parts. Some 220 of these are extra large (180 sq.m) and fully serviced with electricity, water, drainage and TV hook-up. On-site activities include an outdoor water slide complex, an indoor pool, tennis courts and pony riding (all free). A wellness spa centre including a pirate-themed indoor play hall is a recent addition. For children there are numerous play areas, an adventure playground with aerial cable ride and a roller skating area. There is a kayak school and a large bouncy castle for toddlers. Live music and dancing are organised twice a week in high season. Suggested excursions include trips to offshore islands, visits to local potteries, a brewery museum and birdwatching on the Bygholm Vejle.

You might like to know

There is a bird reserve nearby and several inland lakes with fishing trips available.

☑ Beach on site
○ Beach within 1 km
☑ Sandy beach
☑ Blue Flag quality
○ Lifeguard *(high season)*
○ Sun lounger and/or deckchair hire
○ Watersports *(e.g. sailing or windsurfing)*
○ Snacks and drinks
○ Sunshades/sunbeds
○ Dogs allowed *(on the beach)*

Facilities: Two good, large, heated toilet blocks are central, with spacious showers and some washbasins in cubicles. Separate room for children. Baby rooms. Bathrooms for families (some charged) and disabled visitors. Laundry. Well equipped kitchens and barbecue areas. TV lounges. Motorcaravan services. Pizzeria. Supermarket, restaurant and bar (all season). Pool complex. Wellness centre with sauna, solariums, whirlpool bath, fitness room and indoor play hall. TV rental. Play areas. Crèche. Bicycle hire. Cabins to rent. WiFi over part of site (charged). Off site: Golf 10 km. Boat launching 25 km.

Open: 30 March - 21 October.

Directions: Turn off Thisted-Fjerritslev 11 road to Klim from where site is signed.
GPS: 57.133333, 9.166667

Charges guide

Per unit incl. 2 persons and electricity	€ 31,00 - € 50,30
extra person	€ 11,00
child (1-11 yrs)	€ 8,20

Facilities: Superb central toilet block includes washbasins in cubicles, controllable showers, family bathrooms (some with whirlpools and double showers), baby room and excellent facilities for disabled visitors. Excellent kitchen and laundry. Additional facilities to the far end of the site. Motorcaravan services. Supermarket. Restaurant. Takeaway. Indoor and outdoor swimming pools with flumes and slides. Solarium. Well equipped, fenced toddler play area and separate adventure playground. TV and games rooms. Internet café and WiFi. Barbecue area. Fishing. Minigolf. Off site: Beach adjacent. Bicycle hire and riding 10 km. Golf 12 km.

Open: 14 March - 20 October.

Directions: From Fåborg follow 8 road to Bøjden and site is on right 500 m. before ferry terminal (from Fynshav).
GPS: 55.105289, 10.107808

Charges guide

Per unit incl. 2 persons, 1 child and electricity DKK	225 - 385
extra child DKK	65

Credit cards accepted with 5% surcharge.

Denmark – Fåborg

Bøjden Strand Ferie Park

Bøjden Landevej 12, Bøjden, DK-5600 Fåborg (Fyn)
t: 63 60 63 60 e: info@bojden.dk
alanrogers.com/DK2200 www.bojden.dk

Accommodation: ☑ Pitch ☑ Mobile home/chalet ○ Hotel/B&B ○ Apartment

Bøjden is located in one of the most beautiful corners of southwest Fyn (Funen in English), known as the Garden of Denmark, and may well be considered one of the most complete campsites in the country. With just a hedge separating it from the beach, it is suitable for an entire holiday, while remaining a very good centre for excursions. Arranged in rows on mainly level, grassy terraces and divided into groups by hedges and some trees, many pitches have sea views as the site slopes gently down from the road. The 295 pitches (210 for touring) all have electricity (10A) and include 65 new, fully serviced pitches (water, drainage and TV aerial point). Four special motorcaravan pitches also have water and waste points. There are indoor and outdoor pools, the latter with a paddling pool and sun terrace open during suitable weather conditions. Everyone will enjoy the beach (Blue Flag) for swimming, boating and watersports. The water is too shallow for shore fishing but boat trips can be arranged.

You might like to know

The campsite has its own kayak school, a modern indoor and outdoor pool complex and is convenient for day trips to Faaborg, a wonderful old seaport.

- ☑ Beach on site
- ○ Beach within 1 km
- ○ Sandy beach
- ☑ Blue Flag quality
- ○ Lifeguard *(high season)*
- ○ Sun lounger and/or deckchair hire
- ☑ Watersports *(e.g. sailing or windsurfing)*
- ○ Snacks and drinks
- ○ Sunshades/sunbeds
- ○ Dogs allowed *(on the beach)*

TopCamp Feddet

Feddet 12, DK-4640 Faxe (Sjælland)
t: 56 72 52 06 e: info@feddetcamping.dk
alanrogers.com/DK2255 www.feddetcamping.dk

Accommodation: ☑ Pitch ☑ Mobile home/chalet ○ Hotel/B&B ○ Apartment

This interesting, spacious site with ecological principles is located on the Baltic coast. It has a fine, white, sandy beach (Blue Flag) which runs the full length of one side, with the Præstø fjord on the opposite side of the peninsula. There are 413 pitches for touring units, generally on sandy grass, with mature pine trees giving adequate shade. All have 10A electricity and 20 are fully serviced (water, electricity, drainage and sewerage). The sanitary buildings have been specially designed, clad with larch panels from sustainable local trees and insulated with flax mats. They have natural ventilation, controlled by sensors for heat, humidity and smell. Shaped blades on the roof increase ventilation on windy days. All this saves power and provides a comfortable climate inside. Heating, by a wood chip furnace (backed up by a rapeseed oil furnace), is CO_2 neutral and replaces 40,000 litres of heating oil annually. Rainwater is used for toilet flushing, but showers and basins are supplied from the normal mains, and urinals are water free. Water saving taps have an automatic turn off, and lighting is by low wattage bulbs with PIR switching.

Facilities: Both sanitary buildings are equipped to high standards. Family bathrooms (with twin showers), complete suites for children and babies. Facilities for disabled visitors. Laundry. Kitchens, dining room and TV lounge. Excellent motorcaravan service point. Well stocked licensed shop. Licensed bistro and takeaway (1/5-20/10; weekends only outside peak season). Large, indoor swimming pool and paddling pool (charged). Minigolf. Games room. Indoor playroom and several playgrounds. Event camp for children. Pet zoo. Massage. Watersports. Fishing. WiFi. Off site: Abseiling and pool. Amusement park.

Open: All year.

Directions: From south on E47/55 take exit 38 towards Præsto. Turn north on 209 road towards Faxe and from Vindbyholt follow site signs. From the north on E47/55 take exit 37 east towards Faxe. Just before Faxe turn south on 209 road and from Vindbyholt, site signs.

GPS: 55.17497, 12.10203

Charges guide

Per unit incl. 2 persons and electricity	DKK 265 - 340
extra person	DKK 75
child (0-11 yrs)	DKK 55
dog	DKK 20

You might like to know

For something completely different, why not try your hand at abseiling?

☑ Beach on site
○ Beach within 1 km
☑ Sandy beach
☑ Blue Flag quality
○ Lifeguard *(high season)*
○ Sun lounger and/or deckchair hire
○ Watersports *(e.g. sailing or windsurfing)*
○ Snacks and drinks
○ Sunshades/sunbeds
○ Dogs allowed *(on the beach)*

Kawan Village l'Amfora

Avenida Josep Tarradellas, 2, E-17470 Sant Pere Pescador (Girona)
t: 972 520 540 e: info@campingamfora.com
alanrogers.com/ES80350 www.campingamfora.com

Accommodation: ☑ Pitch ☑ Mobile home/chalet ○ Hotel/B&B ☑ Apartment

This spacious site is family run and friendly. It is spotlessly clean and well maintained and the owner operates in an environmentally friendly way. There are 830 level, grass pitches (741 for touring units) laid out in a grid system, all with 10A electricity. Attractive trees and shrubs have been planted around each pitch. There is good shade in the more mature areas, which include 64 large pitches (180 sq.m), each with an individual sanitary unit (toilet, shower and washbasin). The newer area is more open with less shade and you can choose which you would prefer. Access around the site is generally good for disabled visitors. At the entrance, which is hard surfaced with car parking, a terraced bar and two restaurants overlook a smart pool complex with three pools for children, one with two water slides. Alongside the site, the magnificent sandy beach on the Bay of Roses offers good conditions for children and a choice of watersports. A bicycle is useful.

You might like to know

There is a large beach club bar, a kite- and windsurfing school and catamarans for hire on the beach.

☑ Beach on site
○ Beach within 1 km
☑ Sandy beach
☑ Blue Flag quality
☑ Lifeguard *(high season)*
○ Sun lounger and/or deckchair hire
☑ Watersports *(e.g. sailing or windsurfing)*
☑ Snacks and drinks
○ Sunshades/sunbeds
☑ Dogs allowed *(on the beach)*

Facilities: Three main toilet blocks, one heated, provide washbasins in cabins and roomy free showers. Baby rooms. Laundry facilities and service. Motorcaravan services. Supermarket. Terraced bar, self-service and waiter-service restaurants. Pizzeria/takeaway. Restaurant and bar on the beach with limited menu (high season). Disco bar. Swimming pools (1/5-27/9). Pétanque. Tennis. Bicycle hire. Minigolf. Play area. Miniclub. Entertainment and activities. Windsurfing. Kite surfing (low season). Boat launching and sailing. Fishing. Exchange facilities. Games and TV rooms. Internet room and WiFi over site (charged). Car wash. Torches required in beach areas. Off site: Riding 4 km. Golf 15 km.

Open: 14 April - 27 September.

Directions: From north on A17/E15 take exit 3 on N11 towards Figueres and then shortly on C260 towards Roses. At Castello d'Empúries turn right on GIV6216 to Sant Pere. From south on A17 use exit 5 (L'Escala) and turn to Sant Pere in Viladamat. Site is well signed in town.

GPS: 42.18147, 3.10405

Charges guide

Per unit incl. 2 persons and electricity	€ 26,00 - € 60,00
extra person	€ 4,50 - € 6,20
child (2-9 yrs)	€ 2,50 - € 4,20
dog	€ 2,70 - € 5,20

Senior citizen specials.
No credit cards.

Facilities: Five excellent large toilet blocks with electronic sliding glass doors (resident cleaners 07.00-21.00). British style toilets but no seats, controllable hot showers and washbasins in cabins. Excellent facilities for youngsters, babies and disabled campers. Laundry facilities. Motorcaravan services. Extensive supermarket, boutique and other shops. Large bar with terrace. Large restaurant. Takeaway and terrace. Ice cream parlour. Beach bar in main season. Disco club. Swimming pools. New adventure crazy golf. Playgrounds. Tennis. Archery (occasionally). Minigolf. Sailing/windsurfing school and other watersports. Programme of sports, games, excursions and entertainment, partly in English (15/6-31/8). Exchange facilities. ATM. Safety deposit. Internet café. WiFi over site (charged). Dogs taken in one section. Torches required in some areas. Off site: Resort of L'Escala 5 km. Riding and boat launching 5 km. Water park 10 km. Golf 30 km.

Open: 17 May - 19 September.

Directions: L'Escala is northeast of Girona on coast between Palamós and Roses. From A7/E15 autostrada take exit 5 towards L'Escala on GI623. Turn north 2 km. before L'Escala towards Sant Marti d'Ampúrias. Well signed.
GPS: 42.16098, 3.107774

Charges guide

Per unit incl. 2 persons and electricity	€ 22,50 - € 68,00
extra person	€ 3,50 - € 6,00
child (3-10 yrs)	€ 3,00 - € 3,50
dog	€ 3,20 - € 5,00

Spain – Sant Pere Pescador

Camping Las Dunas

Ctra San Marti-Sant Pere, E-17470 Sant Pere Pescador (Girona)
t: 972 521 717   e: info@campinglasdunas.com
alanrogers.com/ES80400   www.campinglasdunas.com

Accommodation: ☑ Pitch   ☑ Mobile home/chalet   ○ Hotel/B&B   ○ Apartment

Las Dunas is an extremely large, impressive and well organised resort-style site with many on-site activities and an ongoing programme of improvements. It has direct access to a superb sandy beach that stretches along the site for nearly a kilometre with a windsurfing school and beach bar. There is also a much used, huge swimming pool, plus a large double pool for children. Las Dunas is very large, with 1,700 individual hedged pitches (1,500 for touring units) of around 100 sq.m. laid out on flat ground in long, regular parallel rows. All have electricity (6/10A) and 180 also have water and drainage. Shade is available in some parts of the site. Pitches are usually available, even in the main season. Much effort has gone into planting palms and new trees here and the results are very attractive. The large restaurant and bar have spacious terraces overlooking the swimming pools or you can enjoy a very pleasant, more secluded, cavern-style pub. A magnificent disco club is close by in a soundproofed building (although people returning from this during the night can be a problem for pitches in the central area of the site). A popular site for British rallies.

You might like to know

Adjacent to the site is the 3 km. golden sandy beach of Sant Pere Pescador. It is a unique landscape bordered by soft dunes.

☑ Beach on site
○ Beach within 1 km
☑ Sandy beach
○ Blue Flag quality
○ Lifeguard *(high season)*
○ Sun lounger and/or deckchair hire
☑ Watersports *(e.g. sailing or windsurfing)*
○ Snacks and drinks
○ Sunshades/sunbeds
○ Dogs allowed *(on the beach)*

Camping la Ballena Alegre

Ctra Sant Marti d'Empuries s/n, E-17470 Sant Pere Pescador (Girona)
t: 972 520 302 e: info@ballena-alegre.com
alanrogers.com/ES80600 www.ballena-alegre.com

Accommodation: ☑ Pitch ☑ Mobile home/chalet ○ Hotel/B&B ○ Apartment

La Ballena Alegre is a spacious site with almost 2 km. of frontage directly onto an excellent beach of soft golden sand (which is cleaned daily). They claim that none of the 966 touring pitches is more than 100 m. from the beach. The grass pitches are individually numbered, many separated by hedges, and there is a choice of size (up to 120 sq.m). Electrical connections (5/10A) are available in all areas and there are 670 fully serviced pitches. There are several bungalow areas within the site with their own small pools and play areas, and some have shared jacuzzis. This is a great site for families. There are restaurant and bar areas beside the pleasant terraced pool complex (four pools including a pool for children). For those who wish to drink and snack late there is a pub open until 03.00. The well managed, soundproofed disco is popular with youngsters. A little train ferries people along the length of the site and a road train runs to local villages. Plenty of entertainment and activities are offered, including a well managed watersports centre, with sub-aqua, windsurfing and kite-surfing, where equipment can be hired and lessons taken.

Facilities: Seven well maintained toilet blocks are of a very high standard. Facilities for children, babies and disabled campers. Launderette. Motorcaravan services. Gas supplies. A comprehensive range of restaurants, snack bars and takeaways, including a pizzeria/trattoria, arroceria, a pub, a self-service restaurant and a beach bar in high season. Swimming pool complex. Jacuzzi. Tennis. Watersports centre. Fitness centre. Bicycle hire. Playgrounds. Soundproofed disco. Dancing twice weekly and organised activities, sports, entertainment, etc. ATM. Dogs only allowed in one zone. Internet and WiFi (charged). Torches useful in beach areas. Off site: Go-karting nearby with bus service. Fishing 300 m. Riding 2 km.

Open: 17 May - 21 September.

Directions: From A7 Figueres-Girona autopista take exit 5 to L'Escala GI623 for 18.5 km. At roundabout take sign to Sant Marti d'Empúries and follow site signs.
GPS: 42.15323, 3.11248

Charges guide

Per unit incl. 2 persons and electricity	€ 26,50 - € 57,00
extra person	€ 4,00 - € 5,00
child (3-10 yrs)	€ 2,80 - € 3,30
dog	€ 2,30 - € 4,80

Discount of 10% on pitch charge for pensioners all season. No credit cards.

You might like to know

The site has a well stocked beach shop so you can make the most of the 1,800 m. long sandy beach.

☑ Beach on site
○ Beach within 1 km
☑ Sandy beach
○ Blue Flag quality
○ Lifeguard *(high season)*
○ Sun lounger and/or deckchair hire
☑ Watersports *(e.g. sailing or windsurfing)*
○ Snacks and drinks
○ Sunshades/sunbeds
○ Dogs allowed *(on the beach)*

Facilities: Very modern, fully equipped, heated sanitary blocks are kept spotlessly clean by omnipresent cleaners. Baby baths and brilliant facilities for children. Washing machines and dryers. Shop, extensive modern complex of restaurants, bars and takeaways (all open all season). Infinity pool (June onwards, lifeguard). Pool bar. Play areas. Kayak hire. Bicycle hire. Organised activities for children in high season. Diving school. Sports centre. WiFi over site (charged). ATM. Private access to beach. Off site: Road train to town centre from outside site. Cala Montgó beach 100 m. GR92 coastal path 50 m. Fishing 150 m. Riding 2 km. Golf 10 km.

Open: 11 March - 20 October.

Directions: From north on A7 take exit 3 to N11, then C31 and GI 623 signed l'Escala. From south take exit 5 from A7 signed l'Escala. Site is clearly marked from town.
GPS: 42.11051, 3.16542

Charges guide

Per unit incl. 2 persons and electricity	€ 24,30 - € 51,25
extra person	€ 3,50 - € 6,90
child (3-10 yrs)	€ 2,45 - € 4,75
dog	€ 2,55 - € 4,35

No credit cards.

Spain – L'Escala

Camping Illa Mateua

Avenida de Montgó 260, E-17130 L'Escala (Girona)
t: 972 770 200   e: info@campingillamateua.com
alanrogers.com/ES80740   www.campingillamateua.com

Accommodation: ☑ Pitch   ☑ Mobile home/chalet   ○ Hotel/B&B   ○ Apartment

If you prefer a quieter site, out of the very busy resort of L'Escala, then Illa Mateua is an excellent option. This large, family run site has a dynamic owner Marti, who speaks excellent English. The site is divided by the beach access road and has its own private accesses to the contrasting beaches – one a rocky cove and the other gentle, sandy and sloping. There are 350 pitches across both parts of the site, all with 6A electricity, some on sloping ground, although the pitches in the second part are flat. Established pine trees provide shade for most places with more coverage on the western side. A new purpose-built diving centre and club opened on the site in 2013. There are two swimming pools, the largest an infinity pool, enjoying an idyllic and most unusual setting on the top of a cliff overlooking the Bay of Roses. The second pool in the bar, restaurant and terrace area is scheduled for redevelopment in 2014. A CCTV system monitors the pools and general security from a purpose built centre.

You might like to know

The beach has hammocks and pedaloes for hire, and there is good access for disabled visitors.

☑ Beach on site
○ Beach within 1 km
☑ Sandy beach
☑ Blue Flag quality
○ Lifeguard (high season)
○ Sun lounger and/or deckchair hire
☑ Watersports (e.g. sailing or windsurfing)
○ Snacks and drinks
☑ Sunshades/sunbeds
○ Dogs allowed (on the beach)

Facilities: Generous sanitary provision. One block is heated in winter. Laundry facilities. Motorcaravan services. Gas supplies. Shop (5/4-30/10). Restaurant (1/2-31/12). Bar, patio bar with pizzas and takeaway (5/4-24/10, weekends for the rest of the year). Swimming pools (26/3-16/10). Playground. Electronic games. Disco two nights a week (but not late) in high season. Bicycle hire. Tennis. Hairdresser. ATM. WiFi (free in hotspots). Torches necessary in some areas. Road train from the bottom of the site to the top in high season.
Off site: Bus at the gate. Beach and fishing 300 m. Supermarket 500 m. Sailing 1 km. Golf 3 km. Riding 10 km.

Open: All year.

Directions: Site is on the inland side of the coast road between Palamós and Platja d'Aro. Take C31 south to 661 at Calonge. At Calonge follow signs to C253 towards Platja d'Aro and on to site, which is well signed.

GPS: 41.83333, 3.08417

Charges guide

Per unit incl. 2 persons and electricity	€ 22,10 - € 51,45
extra person	€ 3,85 - € 8,85
child (3-10 yrs)	€ 1,90 - € 4,80
dog	€ 3,35 - € 4,60

Discounts for longer stays Oct-end May and senior citizens. No credit cards.

Camping Internacional de Calonge

Ctra San Feliu/Guixols - Palamós km 7.6, E-17251 Calonge (Girona)
t: 972 651 233 e: info@intercalonge.com
alanrogers.com/ES81300 www.intercalonge.com

Accommodation: ☑ Pitch ☑ Mobile home/chalet ○ Hotel/B&B ○ Apartment

This spacious, well laid out site has access to a fine beach via a footbridge over the coast road. Calonge is a family site with two attractive pools on different levels, a paddling pool and large sunbathing areas. A restaurant, bar and snack bar with great views are by the pool. The 466 touring pitches are on terraces and all have electricity (5A), with 84 being fully serviced. There is good shade from the tall pine trees, and some spectacular coastal views. Some access roads and steps are steep, but a road train operates in high season. There are wonderful views from the upper levels, where there are some larger comfort pitches. The pools are overlooked by the restaurant terraces which have great views over the mountains. A nature area within the site is used for walks and picnics and two separate areas within the site are set aside for visitors with dogs (dog shower included!). The beach is accessed over the main road by 100 steps.

You might like to know

Visit magical cities such as Barcelona, Girona and Figueres, where you can choose from a vast range of cultural, sporting and leisure activities. Or get away from it all with a walk on the beautiful coastal path.

○ Beach on site
☑ Beach within 1 km
☑ Sandy beach
☑ Blue Flag quality
☑ Lifeguard *(high season)*
○ Sun lounger and/or deckchair hire
☑ Watersports *(e.g. sailing or windsurfing)*
☑ Snacks and drinks
○ Sunshades/sunbeds
○ Dogs allowed *(on the beach)*

Camping Cala Llevadó

Ctra GI-682 de Tossa-Lloret km. 18,9, E-17320 Tossa de Mar (Girona)
t: 972 340 314   e: info@calallevado.com
alanrogers.com/ES82000   www.calallevado.com

Accommodation: ☑ Pitch   ☑ Mobile home/chalet   ○ Hotel/B&B   ○ Apartment

Cala Llevado is a beautifully situated and quiet (although popular), cliff-side site, enjoying fine views of the sea and coast below. It is shaped around a wooded valley with steep access roads and terracing. High up on the site with a superb aspect is the attractive restaurant/bar with a large terrace overlooking the pleasant swimming pool directly below. There are 560 terraced, level touring pitches (489 with 10/16A electricity) on the upper levels of the two slopes, with a great many individual pitches for tents scattered around the site. Many of these pitches have fantastic settings and views. The site is unsuitable for campers with disabilities. In some areas cars may be required to park separately. There are 45 tour operator pitches, 34 bungalows and six new glamping cabins. One beach is for all manner of watersports within a buoyed area and there is a sub-aqua diving school. There are three other pleasant coves, including a naturist area, that can be reached by climbing down on foot (with care!).

You might like to know

There are some beautiful beaches within easy reach, in one of the most scenic parts of the Costa Brava.

- ☑ Beach on site
- ○ Beach within 1 km
- ☑ Sandy beach
- ○ Blue Flag quality
- ○ Lifeguard *(high season)*
- ○ Sun lounger and/or deckchair hire
- ☑ Watersports *(e.g. sailing or windsurfing)*
- ☑ Snacks and drinks
- ○ Sunshades/sunbeds
- ○ Dogs allowed *(on the beach)*

Facilities: Four very well equipped toilet blocks are immaculately maintained and well spaced around the site. Baby baths. Laundry facilities. Motorcaravan services. Gas supplies. Fridge hire. Large supermarket. Restaurant/bar, swimming and paddling pools (all season). Three play areas. Small botanical garden. Entertainment for children and adults (July/Aug). Sports courts. Sailing, water skiing, windsurfing, diving, canoe hire. Fishing. Bicycle hire. Excursions. ATM. Internet access and WiFi over part of site (charged). Torches required in some areas. Doctor service in high season. Only electric barbecues permiited. Off site: Tossa de Mar 3 km.

Open: 1 April - 30 September.

Directions: Leave the AP7/E15 at exit 7 to the C65 Sant Feliu road and then take C35 southeast to the GI681 to Tossa de Mar. Site is signed off the GI682 Lloret-Tossa road at km. 18,9, 3 km. from Tossa. Route avoids the difficult coastal road.

GPS: 41.71292, 2.906465

Charges guide

Per unit incl. 2 persons and electricity	€ 26,05 - € 52,00
extra person	€ 6,35 - € 9,25
child (4-12 yrs)	€ 3,65 - € 5,75
dog	€ 5,10 - € 5,45

Camping Resort Sanguli Salou

Passeig Miramar-Plaça Venus, Apdo 123, E-43840 Salou (Tarragona)
t: 977 381 641 e: mail@sanguli.es
alanrogers.com/ES84800 www.sanguli.es

Accommodation: ☑ Pitch ☑ Mobile home/chalet ○ Hotel/B&B ○ Apartment

Facilities: The six sanitary blocks are constantly cleaned and are always exceptional, including many individual cabins with en-suite facilities. Improvements are made each year. Some blocks have excellent facilities for babies. Launderette with service. Motorcaravan services. Car wash (charged). Gas supplies. Snack bars. Indoor and outdoor restaurants with takeaway. Swimming pools. Fitness centre. Sports complex. Fitness room (charged). Playgrounds including adventure play area. Miniclub. Minigolf. Multiple Internet options including WiFi (free). Security bracelets. Medical centre.
Off site: Activities on the beach 50 m. Bus at gate. Bicycle hire 100 m. Fishing 200 m. Riding 3 km. Port Aventura 4 km. Aquopolis and golf 5 km.

Open: 20 March - 2 November.

Directions: On west side of Salou 1 km. from the centre, site is well signed from the coast road to Cambrils and from the other town approaches.
GPS: 41.07546, 1.11651

Charges guide

Per unit incl. 2 persons and electricity	€ 29,00 - € 78,00
extra person	€ 7,00
child (4-12 yrs)	€ 5,00

Reductions outside high season for longer stays. Special long stay offers for senior citizens.

Camping Resort Sanguli Salou is a superb site boasting excellent pools and entertainment. Owned, developed and managed by a local Spanish family, it has something for all the family with everything open when the site is open. There are 1,089 pitches of varying sizes (75-120 sq.m) all with electricity (7.5-10A). Mobile homes occupy 58 pitches and there are fully equipped bungalows on 147. A wonderful selection of trees, palms and shrubs provide natural shade and an ideal space for children to play. The good sandy beach is little more than 50 metres across the coast road and a small railway crossing. Although large, Sanguli has a pleasant, open feel and maintains a quality family atmosphere due to the efforts of the very keen and efficient staff. There are three very attractive themed pools, which include water slides and elephants. Amenities include a children's play park, organised activities for adults and children, a miniclub, tennis courts, table tennis, minigolf, a football pitch, volleyball, and a fitness room. This is a large, professional site providing something for all the family, but still capable of providing peace and quiet for those looking for it.

You might like to know

Activities on the beach include windsurfing, sailing, water skiing, pedaloes and, 800 m. from here, sea fishing. The attractive seafront promenade will take you into the centre of Salou.

○ Beach on site
☑ Beach within 1 km
☑ Sandy beach
☑ Blue Flag quality
☑ Lifeguard *(high season)*
☑ Sun lounger and/or deckchair hire
☑ Watersports *(e.g. sailing or windsurfing)*
☑ Snacks and drinks
☑ Sunshades/sunbeds
○ Dogs allowed *(on the beach)*

Facilities: Five very well maintained, fully equipped, toilet blocks include units for disabled visitors and babies and new facilities for children. Washing machines. Gas supplies. Large supermarket, bakery and souvenir shops at entrance, open to public. Full restaurant. Takeaway. Bar with large terrace where entertainment is held daily. Beach bar. Coffee bar and ice-cream bar. Pizzeria. Open-roof cinema with permanent seating for 520. 3 TV lounges. Soundproofed disco. Swimming pools (two heated). Solarium. Sauna. Two large jacuzzis. Seawater jacuzzi and Turkish sauna. Sports areas. Tennis. Squash. Language school (Spanish). Minigolf. Sub-aqua diving (first dive free). Bicycle hire. Fishing. Windsurfing school. Sailboards and pedaloes for hire. Playground, crèche and Happy Camp. Fridge hire. Library. Hairdresser. Business centre. WiFi. Car repair and car wash (pressure wash). No animals permitted. No jet skis accepted. Off site: Buses on N340 close to site. Port Aventura. Beach fishing. Riding 3 km. Golf 4 km.

Open: 15 March - 31 October.

Directions: Entrance is off main N340 road by 1136 km. marker, 30 km. from Tarragona towards Valencia. From motorway take Cambrils exit and turn west on N340.

GPS: 41.03707, 0.97478

Charges guide

Per unit incl. 2 persons and electricity	€ 20,30 - € 66,55
extra person	€ 3,35 - € 9,90
child (0-10 yrs)	no charge - € 7,85

Discounts in low season for longer stays.

Spain – Montroig

Camping La Torre del Sol

Ctra N340 km. 1136, E-43300 Montroig (Tarragona)
t: 977 810 486 e: info@latorredelsol.com
alanrogers.com/ES85400 www.latorredelsol.com

Accommodation: ☑ Pitch ☑ Mobile home/chalet ☑ Hotel/B&B ○ Apartment

A pleasant banana tree-lined approach road gives way to avenues of palms as you arrive at Torre del Sol. This is a very large, well designed site occupying a good position in the south of Catalunya with direct access to the soft sand beach. The site is exceptionally well maintained by a large workforce. There is good shade on a high proportion of the 1,500 individual, numbered pitches (700 for touring). All have electricity and are mostly of about 90 sq.m. Strong features are 800 m. of clean beachfront, three attractive pools with two jacuzzis in the bar and restaurant area. A new seawater jacuzzi and Turkish sauna were opened in 2012. Occasional train noise on some pitches. The cinema doubles as a theatre to stage shows all season. The complex of three pools, thoughtfully laid out with grass sunbathing areas and palms, has a lifeguard. We were impressed with the provision of season-long entertainment, giving parents a break whilst children were in the safe hands of the activities team, who ensure they enjoy the novel Happy Camp and various workshops.

You might like to know

The campsite has its own private beach, which is cleaned daily and hosts regular games and entertainment.

- ☑ Beach on site
- ○ Beach within 1 km
- ☑ Sandy beach
- ○ Blue Flag quality
- ○ Lifeguard *(high season)*
- ○ Sun lounger and/or deckchair hire
- ☑ Watersports *(e.g. sailing or windsurfing)*
- ○ Snacks and drinks
- ○ Sunshades/sunbeds
- ○ Dogs allowed *(on the beach)*

Facilities: Six excellent, spacious and fully equipped toilet blocks include baby baths. Large laundry. Motorcaravan services. Gas supplies. Freezer service. Supermarket. General shop. Kiosk. Restaurant and bar. Takeaway (July/Aug). Swimming pools, bathing caps compulsory (20/5-15/9). Entertainment organised with a soundproofed pub/disco (July/Aug). Tennis. Gym park. Playground. Riding. Fishing. Nature animal park. Hairdresser (July/Aug). Medical centre. Torches necessary in some areas. Animals are not accepted. WiFi on part of site (charged). Off site: Bicycle hire and large sports complex with multiple facilities including an indoor pool 1 km. Sailing and boat launching 10 km. Riding and golf 20 km.

Open: 27 March - 27 September.

Directions: From A8 (Bilbao-Santander) take km. 185 exit and N634 towards Beranga. Almost immediately turn right on CA147 to Noja. In 10 km. turn left at multiple campsite signs and go through town. At beach follow signs to site.

GPS: 43.48948, -3.53700

Charges guide

Per unit incl. 2 persons and electricity	€ 28,90 - € 49,20
extra person	€ 4,50 - € 7,00
child (3-9 yrs)	€ 3,15 - € 5,10

Spain – Noja

Camping Playa Joyel

Playa de Ris, E-39180 Noja (Cantabria)
t: 942 630 081 e: info@playjoyel.com
alanrogers.com/ES90000 www.playajoyel.com

Accommodation: ☑ Pitch ☑ Mobile home/chalet ○ Hotel/B&B ○ Apartment

This very attractive holiday and touring site is some 40 kilometres from Santander and 80 kilometres from Bilbao. It is a busy, high quality, comprehensively equipped site by a superb beach providing 1,000 well shaded, marked and numbered pitches with 6A electricity available. These include 80 large pitches of 100 sq.m. Some 250 pitches are occupied by tour operators and seasonal units. This well managed site has a lot to offer for family holidays with much going on in high season when it gets crowded. The swimming pool complex (with lifeguard) is free to campers and the superb beaches are cleaned daily mid-June to mid-September. Two beach exits lead to the main beach where there are some undertows, or if you turn left you will find a reasonably placid estuary. An unusual feature here is the nature park within the site boundary which has a selection of animals to see. This overlooks a protected area of marsh where European birds spend the winter.

You might like to know

The fine sandy beach, which is excellent for surfing, is cleaned daily. At low tide there are warm pools for splashing in and rock pools with small fish and crabs.

- ☑ Beach on site
- ○ Beach within 1 km
- ☑ Sandy beach
- ○ Blue Flag quality
- ○ Lifeguard *(high season)*
- ○ Sun lounger and/or deckchair hire
- ☑ Watersports *(e.g. sailing or windsurfing)*
- ○ Snacks and drinks
- ○ Sunshades/sunbeds
- ○ Dogs allowed *(on the beach)*

Facilities: The modern shower/WC blocks also provide male and female saunas, kitchen and launderette facilities. Facilities for disabled visitors. Motorcaravan services. Playground. Reception with café/restaurant (June-Aug), souvenir and grocery shop. TV room. Free WiFi over site. Bicycle hire. Communal barbecues only. Off site: The adjacent Eden Centre provides excellent modern spa facilities where you can enjoy a day under the glass-roofed pool with its jacuzzis, saunas, Turkish baths and an Irish bath. Riding 2 km. Fishing 5 km. Golf 15 km.

Open: All year.

Directions: Leave road 4/E75 at junction with road 20 and head west down Kiertotie. Site well signed, Nallikari Eden, but continue on, just after traffic lights, cross a bridge and take the second on the right. Just before the Eden Centre turn right towards Leiritie and reception.

GPS: 65.02973, 25.41793

Charges guide

Per unit incl. 2 persons € 13,00 - € 26,00	
extra person € 4,00	
child (under 15 yrs) € 2,00	
electricity € 4,50 - € 6,50	

Finland – Oulu

Nallikari Camping

Leiritie 10, FIN-90510 Oulu (Oulu)
t: 044 703 1353 e: nallikari.camping@ouka.fi
alanrogers.com/FI2970 www.nallikari.fi

Accommodation: ☑ Pitch ☑ Mobile home/chalet ○ Hotel/B&B ○ Apartment

This is probably one of the best sites in Scandinavia, set in a recreational wooded area alongside a sandy beach on the banks of the Baltic Sea, with the added bonus of the adjacent Eden Spa complex. Nallikari provides 200 pitches, 176 with 16A electricity (seven also have water supply and drainage), plus an additional 78 cottages to rent, 28 of which are suitable for winter occupation. Oulu is a modern town, about 100 miles south of the Arctic Circle, that enjoys long, sunny and dry summer days. The Baltic, however, is frozen for many weeks in the winter and then the sun barely rises for two months. In early June the days are very long with the sun setting at about 23.30 and rising at 01.30! Nallikari, to the west of Oulu, is 3 km. along purpose-built cycle paths and the town has much to offer. Nordic walking, with or without roller blades, seems to be a recreational pastime for Finns of all ages! You might even be tempted to buy a pair of long, brightly-coloured walking sticks yourself! Oulu hosts events such as the Meri Oulu Festival in July and the Oulu Music Video Festival and forms the backdrop to the mind boggling, air guitar world championships.

You might like to know

Activities on the beach include beach volleyball, and there are beach tennis courts nearby.

- ☑ Beach on site
- ○ Beach within 1 km
- ☑ Sandy beach
- ○ Blue Flag quality
- ○ Lifeguard *(high season)*
- ○ Sun lounger and/or deckchair hire
- ○ Watersports *(e.g. sailing or windsurfing)*
- ○ Snacks and drinks
- ○ Sunshades/sunbeds
- ○ Dogs allowed *(on the beach)*

France – Saint Georges-de-Didonne

Camping Bois Soleil

2 avenue de Suzac, F-17110 Saint Georges-de-Didonne (Charente-Maritime)
t: 05 46 05 05 94   e: camping.bois.soleil@wanadoo.fr
alanrogers.com/FR17010   www.bois-soleil.com

Accommodation: ☑ Pitch ☑ Mobile home/chalet ○ Hotel/B&B ○ Apartment

Facilities: Each area has one large and one small sanitary block. Heated block near reception. Cleaned twice daily, they include facilities for disabled visitors and babies. Launderette. Supermarket, bakery, beach shop (all 15/4-15/9). Restaurant, bar and takeaway (all 15/4-15/9). Swimming pool (heated 15/6-15/9). Steam room. Tennis. Play area. TV room and library. Internet terminal. WiFi throughout (charged). Charcoal and electric barbecues are not permitted. Dogs are not accepted 29/6-25/8. Off site: Bicycle hire adjacent. Fishing 200 m. Riding 500 m. Golf 20 km.

Open: 2 April - 9 October.

Directions: From Royan centre take coast road (D25) along the seafront of St Georges-de-Didonne towards Meschers. Site is signed at roundabout at end of the main beach.

GPS: 45.583583, -0.986533

Charges guide

Per unit incl. 3 persons and electricity	€ 16,00 - € 47,00
extra person	€ 6,00 - € 12,00
child (under 7 yrs)	no charge - € 8,00
dog (not 29/6-25/8)	€ 3,00 - € 5,00

Close to the sea, Bois Soleil is a large site in three parts, with 165 serviced pitches for touring units and a few for tents. All the touring pitches are hedged and have electricity (all 10A), with water and drainage between two. The main part, Les Pins, is attractive with trees and shrubs providing shade. Opposite is La Mer with direct access to the beach, some areas with less shade and an area for tents. The third part, La Forêt, is for caravan holiday homes. It is best to book your preferred area as it can be full mid June to late August. Excellent private sanitary facilities are available to rent, either on your pitch or at a block (subject to availability). There are a few pitches with lockable gates. The areas are all well tended and are cleared and raked between visitors. This lively site offers something for everyone, whether it be a beach-side spot or a traditional pitch, plenty of activities or the quiet life. Recent additions include a new toilet block and some accommodation to rent with sea views. The wide sandy beach is popular with children and provides a pleasant walk to the pretty town of Saint Georges-de-Didonne.

You might like to know

There are plenty of opportunities to sample the regional specialities – seafood, oysters from Marennes-Oléron, Cognac and the well known Pineau des Charentes.

- ☑ Beach on site
- ○ Beach within 1 km
- ☑ Sandy beach
- ☑ Blue Flag quality
- ☑ Lifeguard *(high season)*
- ○ Sun lounger and/or deckchair hire
- ☑ Watersports *(e.g. sailing or windsurfing)*
- ☑ Snacks and drinks
- ☑ Sunshades/sunbeds
- ○ Dogs allowed *(on the beach)*

Facilities: Traditional style toilet facilities are kept to a high standard and include provision for disabled visitors. Laundry facilities. Motorcaravan services. Shop with bakery. Restaurant and bar (1/4-15/9). Indoor pool with first class spa and wellness centre (all year, with professional staff). Outdoor pool (heated, 1/4-15/9). Play area. Bicycle hire. Children's clubs and entertainment (July/Aug). Internet access and Free WiFi on part of site. ATM. No charcoal barbecues. Off site: Beach 200 m. and 400 m. via a sandy path. Bus service from Chéray. Fishing 2 km. Riding 2 km. Golf 12 km.

Open: Mid March - 11 November.

Directions: Cross the viaduct onto the Ile d'Oléron. Take D734 (St Georges-d'Oléron). At traffic lights in Chéray turn left. Follow signs for camping and Les Sable Vignier. After prominent speed bumps turn right and follow site signs to les Gros Joncs.

GPS: 45.95356, -1.37979

Charges guide

Per unit incl. 2 persons and electricity	€ 20,30 - € 50,50
extra person	€ 6,80 - € 13,30
child (under 7 yrs)	€ 3,10 - € 8,10
dog	no charge - € 3,00

France – Saint Georges-d'Oléron

Camping les Gros Joncs

Les Sables Vignier B.P. 17, F-17190 Saint Georges-d'Oléron (Charente-Maritime)
t: 05 46 76 52 29   e: info@les-gros-joncs.fr
alanrogers.com/FR17070   www.camping-les-gros-joncs.com

Accommodation: ☑ Pitch ☑ Mobile home/chalet ○ Hotel/B&B ○ Apartment

Situated on the west coast of the island of Ile d'Oléron, les Gros Joncs is owned and run by the Cavel family who work hard to keep the site up to date and of high quality. There are 50 or so touring pitches of a good size (some extra large) with tall pine trees providing a choice between full sun and varying degrees of shade. All have water and 10A electricity to hand. The main building not only houses a light and airy reception, but also a modern, beautifully presented bar and restaurant, a fully stocked and competitively priced shop, an attractive indoor swimming pool and a magnificent spa. The indoor pool, with water jets and jacuzzi, has glass sides which in good weather are opened out onto an outdoor pool area where there are also water slides, a paddling area and plenty of sunbathing terraces. Both pools are heated. The spa offers hydrotherapy and beauty treatments, sauna, and a comprehensive fitness room. Much attention has been given to the needs of disabled visitors here, including chalets where space and equipment are specially adapted. All the amenities are of a standard unusual on a campsite.

You might like to know

Our heated open-air pools include a toboggan, a large swimming pool and an adventure paddling pool. The indoor pool also has a whirlpool, lazy river, anatomical seats and powerful water jets.

☑ Beach on site
○ Beach within 1 km
☑ Sandy beach
○ Blue Flag quality
☑ Lifeguard *(high season)*
○ Sun lounger and/or deckchair hire
○ Watersports *(e.g. sailing or windsurfing)*
○ Snacks and drinks
○ Sunshades/sunbeds
☑ Dogs allowed *(on the beach)*

Facilities:
The unisex, heated sanitary block is first class, with washbasins in cubicles, showers, British style WCs, facilities for children and disabled visitors. Laundry facilities. Shop. Takeaway. Covered swimming pool (heated all season) and jacuzzi. Bicycle hire. Fridge hire. Play area. Games room. Library. TV room. Charcoal barbecues are not permitted. Free WiFi over site. Off site: Beach, fishing, boat launching and sailing 2 km. Bar and restaurant 2 km. Riding 3 km. Golf 10 km.

Open: 4 April - 30 September.

Directions: Follow the signs for St Martin. The site is on the main road between La Flotte and St Martin.

GPS: 46.18755, -1.344933

Charges guide

Per unit incl. 2 persons
and electricity € 21,00 - € 45,00

extra person	€ 5,50 - € 9,00
child (0-7 yrs)	€ 3,50 - € 5,00
dog	€ 3,00 - € 4,50

France – La Flotte-en-Ré

Camping la Grainetière

Route de Saint Martin, Chemin des Essarts, F-17630 La Flotte-en-Ré (Charente-Maritime)
t: 05 46 09 68 86   e: la-grainetiere@orange.fr
alanrogers.com/FR17280   www.la-grainetiere.com

Accommodation: ☑ Pitch ☑ Mobile home/chalet ○ Hotel/B&B ○ Apartment

A truly friendly welcome awaits you from Isabelle, Eric and Fanny at la Grainetière. It is a peaceful campsite set in almost three hectares of pine trees which provide some shade for the 51 touring pitches of various shapes and sizes. There are also 80 well spaced chalets, mobile homes and roulottes for rent. Some pitches are suitable for units up to seven metres (these should be booked in advance). There are no hedges for privacy and the pitches are sandy with some grass. Most pitches have a water point, electricity (10A) and waste water drainage. The site is well lit. At the site entrance there is a very attractive swimming pool surrounded by tropical plants, with plenty of space to sunbathe. There are no toboggans here and the atmosphere is convivial and relaxed. The site is situated just 1.5 kilometres from the beach and La Flotte-en-Ré with its harbour-side restaurants is even closer.

You might like to know

There are some excellent beaches nearby – Arnerault at La Flotte (1.5 km) and Cible at St Martin (2.5 km), while the main resort of Le Bois Plage, on the other side of the island, is just 4.5 km. from the site.

○ Beach on site

○ Beach within 1 km

☑ Sandy beach

○ Blue Flag quality

☑ Lifeguard *(high season)*

○ Sun lounger and/or deckchair hire

☑ Watersports *(e.g. sailing or windsurfing)*

○ Snacks and drinks

○ Sunshades/sunbeds

○ Dogs allowed *(on the beach)*

Facilities: The two toilet blocks are modern and well maintained with facilities for children and disabled visitors. Laundry. Dog shower. Motorcaravan services. Shop. Bar, restaurant and takeaway. Swimming pool (27/4-29/9). Games room. Riding. Tennis. Fishing pond adjacent. Play area. Minigolf (free). Trampolines and bouncy castle. Boules. Multisports area. Entertainment in high season. Bicycle hire. No charcoal barbecues. Internet and WiFi (free). Mobile homes for rent. Spa with sauna, Hammam, jacuzzi etc. Off site: Jet ski hire adjacent. Beach 50 m. La Couarde 2.5 km. Golf 5 km.

Open: 27 April - 28 September.

Directions: After toll bridge, join D735 which runs along the north side of island until you pass La Couarde. The site is 2.5 km. beyond village (towards Ars-en-Ré).

GPS: 46.20433, -1.46767

Charges guide

Per unit incl. 1 or 2 persons and electricity	€ 25,00 - € 49,00
extra person	€ 5,00 - € 11,00
dog	€ 3,00 - € 5,00

France – La Couarde-sur-Mer

Camping l'Océan

50 route d'Ars, F-17670 La Couarde-sur-Mer (Charente-Maritime)
t: 05 46 29 87 70 e: info@campingocean.com
alanrogers.com/FR17230 www.campingocean.com

Accommodation: ☑ Pitch ☑ Mobile home/chalet ◯ Hotel/B&B ◯ Apartment

L'Océan lies close to the centre of the Ile de Ré, just 50 m. from a sandy beach. There are 338 pitches here with 161 for touring units, the remainder occupied by mobile homes and chalets. The camping area is well shaded and pitches are of a reasonable size, all with electricity (10A). A pleasant bar/restaurant overlooks the large heated swimming pool which is surrounded by an attractive sunbathing terrace. Bicycle hire is popular here as the island offers over 100 km. of interesting cycle routes. A bus goes to La Rochelle from 300 metres outside the site. In peak season a range of entertainment is organised including disco evenings.

You might like to know

A fine sand beach is just 50 m. away. With over 100 km. of cycle paths, why not discover the magic of the Ile de Ré by bicycle?

◯ Beach on site
☑ Beach within 1 km
☑ Sandy beach
◯ Blue Flag quality
◯ Lifeguard *(high season)*
◯ Sun lounger and/or deckchair hire
☑ Watersports *(e.g. sailing or windsurfing)*
◯ Snacks and drinks
◯ Sunshades/sunbeds
◯ Dogs allowed *(on the beach)*

Antioche d'Oléron

16 route de Proires, F-17840 La Brée-les-Bains (Charente-Maritime)
t: 05 46 47 92 00   e: info@camping-antiochedoleron.com
alanrogers.com/FR17570   www.camping-antiochedoleron.com

Accommodation: ☑ Pitch   ☑ Mobile home/chalet   ○ Hotel/B&B   ○ Apartment

Facilities: The modern sanitary block is of a good standard and is kept clean and fresh. Cubicle with controllable shower and washbasin. Facilities for babies and disabled visitors. No chemical disposal point (drains on pitches used). Laundry. Bar and snack bar with takeaway. Two heated swimming pools (one will be covered for 2014). Paddling pool. Jacuzzi. Play area. Children's club and evening entertainment and activities for all the family (July/Aug). WiFi over site (charged July/Aug). Bicycle hire. Off site: Beach and fishing 150 m. Village with market (daily 15/6-15/9) 1 km. Riding 1.5 km. Sailing and boat launching 2.5 km. Golf 7 km.

Open: 6 April - 28 September.

Directions: Cross the bridge to the Ile d'Oléron and continue on the D26/D734 through St Pierre and St Georges, then turn right onto the D273E1 towards La Brée-les-Baines. Bear left at roundabout, then at T-junction turn left from where the campsite is signed.
GPS: 46.02007, -1.35764

Charges guide

Per unit incl. 2 persons and electricity	€ 23,10 - € 39,05
extra person	€ 7,75 - € 9,10
child (1-14 yrs)	€ 4,40 - € 5,70
dog	€ 4,30

Close to the northern point of the Ile d'Oléron, Antioche is quietly located within a five minute walk of the beach. There are 130 pitches, of which 87 are occupied by mobile homes, half available for rent, and 43 are for touring units. The pitches are set amongst attractive shrubs and palm trees and all have 16A electricity, water and a drain. The site becomes livelier in season with regular evening entertainment and activities for all the family. A thriving market selling local produce and products is within easy reach on foot, and is held daily in high season. Along the road at Saint Denis-d'Oléron is a busy port and marina with a choice of bars and restaurants, many specialising in seafood including local oysters and mussels. A short drive south takes you to Saint Georges, though for a better choice of shops and restaurants - and a hypermarket - head on to Saint Pierre. There is a good choice of sandy beaches, whilst across the salt marshes at Boyardville you can take out a canoe or go on a boat trip across to historical Fort Boyard, or to the Ile d'Aix.

You might like to know

One area of the beach is dedicated to watersports and pleasure boats. At low tide there is a flat, rocky area, perfect for fishing.

○ Beach on site
☑ Beach within 1 km
☑ Sandy beach
○ Blue Flag quality
☑ Lifeguard *(high season)*
○ Sun lounger and/or deckchair hire
☑ Watersports *(e.g. sailing or windsurfing)*
☑ Snacks and drinks
○ Sunshades/sunbeds
○ Dogs allowed *(on the beach)*

Facilities: Six well placed toilet blocks are of good quality and include washbasins in large cabins and controllable hot showers. One block includes a separate laundry and dog washing enclosures. Baby rooms. Separate facility for disabled visitors. Launderette. Hairdressing room. Motorcaravan services. Well stocked shop. Extensive snack bar and takeaway. Bar with games room and night club. Library/reading room with four computer stations. Entertainment room with satellite TV. Pool complex with indoor and outdoor pools, children's pool, jacuzzi and slide. Fitness centre (no charge). Sauna (charged). Tennis and squash (charged). Boules. Archery. Well equipped play area. Entertainment and activities (July/Aug). WiFi over most of site (charged). Off site: Bicycle hire 150 m. Sailing, fishing, riding and golf all nearby. Bénodet and Quimper.

Open: 19 June - 5 September.

Directions: From N165 take D70 Concarneau exit. At first roundabout take D44 to Fouesnant. Turn right at T-junction. After 2 km. turn left to Fouesnant (still D44). Continue through La Forêt Fouesnant and Fouesnant, picking up signs for Bénodet. Shortly before Bénodet at roundabout turn left (Le Letty). Turn right at next mini-roundabout and site is 500 m. on left.

GPS: 47.86700, -4.08783

Charges guide

Per unit incl. 2 persons and electricity € 24,00 - € 43,00	
extra person € 5,00 - € 10,00	
child (2-6 yrs) € 4,00 - € 7,00	
dog € 2,50 - € 3,20	

France – Bénodet

Camping du Letty

Chemin de Creisanguer, F-29950 Bénodet (Finistère)
t: 02 98 57 04 69   e: reception@campingduletty.com
alanrogers.com/FR29030   www.campingduletty-benodet.com

Accommodation: ☑ Pitch   ○ Mobile home/chalet   ○ Hotel/B&B   ○ Apartment

The Guyader family have ensured that this excellent and attractive site has plenty to offer for all the family. With a charming ambience, the site on the outskirts of the popular resort of Bénodet spreads over 22 acres with 542 pitches, all for touring units. Groups of four to eight pitches are set in cul-de-sacs with mature hedging and trees to divide each group. All pitches have electricity (10A), water and drainage. As well as direct access to a small sandy beach, with a floating pontoon (safe bathing depends on the tides), the site has a grand aquatic parc, with heated open-air and indoor pools including children's pools, jacuzzi, and slides. At the attractive floral entrance, former farm buildings provide a host of facilities including an extensively equipped fitness room and new wellness rooms for massages and jacuzzis. There is also a modern, purpose built nightclub and bar providing high quality live entertainment most evenings (situated well away from most pitches to avoid disturbance).

You might like to know

Letty is beside La Mer Blanche, which empties and fills with the rhythm of the tides and is a haven for birds. The area is a paradise for walkers and nature lovers and has some wonderful sandy beaches.

- ☑ Beach on site
- ○ Beach within 1 km
- ☑ Sandy beach
- ○ Blue Flag quality
- ○ Lifeguard *(high season)*
- ○ Sun lounger and/or deckchair hire
- ☑ Watersports *(e.g. sailing or windsurfing)*
- ☑ Snacks and drinks
- ○ Sunshades/sunbeds
- ☑ Dogs allowed *(on the beach)*

Facilities: Two clean, well maintained sanitary blocks include mixed style toilets, washbasins in cabins, baby baths and facilities for disabled visitors. Laundry room. Motorcaravan services. Small shop (from 15/5). Bar and restaurant (from 1/6) with outside terrace and takeaway. Reading and TV room. Heated indoor and outdoor pools with sun terrace and paddling pool. Sauna (charged). Play areas. Games room. Various activities are organised in July/Aug. Internet access. WiFi (charged). Off site: Beach, fishing and watersports 300 m. Supermarket 3 km. Riding 4 km.

Open: 11 April - 30 September.

Directions: From N165 take D24 Kerampaou exit. After 3 km. turn right towards Nizon and bear right at church in village following signs to Névez (D77). Continue through Névez, following signs to Raguénès. Continue for 3 km. to site entrance on left (entrance is quite small and easy to miss).

GPS: 47.79337, -3.80049

Charges guide

Per unit incl. 2 persons and electricity	€ 20,30 - € 39,70
extra person	€ 4,40 - € 6,00
child (under 7 yrs)	no charge - € 3,90
dog	€ 1,50 - € 3,20

France – Névez

Camping le Raguénès-Plage

19 rue des Iles, F-29920 Névez (Finistère)
t: 02 98 06 80 69 e: leraguenesplage@orange.fr
alanrogers.com/FR29090 www.camping-le-raguenes-plage.com

Accommodation: ☑ Pitch ☑ Mobile home/chalet ○ Hotel/B&B ○ Apartment

Mme. Guyader and her family will ensure you receive a warm welcome on arrival at this well kept and pleasant site. Le Raguénès-Plage is an attractive and well laid out campsite with many shrubs and trees. The 287 pitches are a good size, flat and grassy, separated by trees and hedges. All have electricity, water and drainage. The site is used by two tour operators (51 pitches), and has 61 mobile homes of its own. A pool complex complete with heated indoor pool and water toboggan is a key feature and is close to the friendly bar, restaurant, shop and takeaway. From the far end of the campsite a delightful five minute walk along a path and through a cornfield takes you down to a pleasant, sandy beach looking out towards the Ile Verte and the Presqu'île de Raguénès.

You might like to know

There is a heated, covered pool, and a separate outdoor pool, also heated, with water slide and paddling pool.

- ☑ Beach on site
- ○ Beach within 1 km
- ☑ Sandy beach
- ☑ Blue Flag quality
- ○ Lifeguard *(high season)*
- ○ Sun lounger and/or deckchair hire
- ☑ Watersports *(e.g. sailing or windsurfing)*
- ☑ Snacks and drinks
- ○ Sunshades/sunbeds
- ○ Dogs allowed *(on the beach)*

Facilities: Three toilet blocks provide washbasins in cubicles and showers (token from reception € 0.65-0.85). Facilities for disabled visitors and babies. Fully equipped laundry. Motorcaravan services. Shop stocks essentials (14/5-22/9). Takeaway (July/Aug). Play area. Games room. Hairdresser. The site is famous for its Breton music and dancing, cooking classes and guided walks arranged. Splendid beach with good bathing, fishing, windsurfing and other watersports. WiFi throughout. Off site: Bus service just outside site. Pizzeria next door. Tennis. Sailing club 3 km. Riding 7 km. Golf 30 km. Miles of superb coastal walks. The nearby town of L'Aber Wrac'h, a well known yachting centre, has many restaurants.

Open: 1 May - 30 September.

Directions: Landéda is 55 km. west of Roscoff via D10 to Plougerneau then D13 crossing river bridge (Aber Wrac'h) and turning west to Lannilis. From N12 Morlaix-Brest road turn north on D59 to Lannilis. Continue through town taking road to Landéda and from there follow signs for Dunes de Ste Marguerite, Camping and des Abers.

GPS: 48.59344, -4.60281

Charges guide

Per unit incl. 2 persons and electricity € 15,30 - € 18,00
extra person € 3,40 - € 4,00
child (under 7 yrs) € 2,10 - € 2,50
dog € 1,90 - € 2,20

France – Landéda

Camping des Abers

Dunes de Sainte Marguerite, F-29870 Landéda (Finistère)
t: 02 98 04 93 35 e: camping-des-abers@wanadoo.fr
alanrogers.com/FR29130 www.camping-des-abers.com

Accommodation: ☑ Pitch ☑ Mobile home/chalet ○ Hotel/B&B ○ Apartment

This delightful 12-acre site is in a beautiful location almost at the tip of the Presqu'île Sainte Marguerite on the northwestern shores of Brittany. The peninsula lies between the mouths (abers) of two rivers, Aber Wrac'h and Aber Benoît. Camping des Abers is set just back from a wonderful sandy beach with rocky outcrops and islands you can walk to at low tide. There are 180 pitches (158 for touring), landscaped and terraced, some with amazing views, others sheltered by mature hedges, trees and flowering shrubs. Hubert le Cuff and his team make you very welcome and speak excellent English. This extensive site was created out of nothing by the le Cuff family who have tended it with loving care over the years. It is arranged on different levels avoiding any regimentation or crowding. Easily accessed by good internal roads, electricity is available to all (long leads may be needed). With its soft, white sandy beach the setting is ideal for those with younger children and this quiet, rural area provides a wonderful, tranquil escape from the hustle and bustle of life, even in high season.

You might like to know

There is a sailing club five minutes drive from the site, and on the nearby estuary there are oyster farms and a bird sanctuary.

- ☑ Beach on site
- ○ Beach within 1 km
- ☑ Sandy beach
- ○ Blue Flag quality
- ○ Lifeguard *(high season)*
- ○ Sun lounger and/or deckchair hire
- ☑ Watersports *(e.g. sailing or windsurfing)*
- ○ Snacks and drinks
- ○ Sunshades/sunbeds
- ○ Dogs allowed *(on the beach)*

Facilities: Two modern sanitary blocks, recently completely renewed and heated in winter, include mainly British style toilets, some washbasins in cubicles, baby baths and good facilities for disabled visitors. Family bathrooms. Laundry facilities. Motorcaravan services. Shop. Restaurant by entrance, bar and terrace, takeaway (12/4-15/9). Covered, heated swimming and paddling pools (23/6-26/8). New wellness centre with sauna, steam room and fitness. Large games hall. Play area. Football field. Minigolf. Communal barbecue area. Daily activities for children and adults organised in July/Aug. Bicycle hire. Internet access and WiFi in reception area (charged). Off site: Nearby sea and river fishing and watersports. Beach 250 m. Riding 2 km. Golf 15 km.

Open: 11 April - 20 September.

Directions: From N165 take either exit for Kervidanou, Quimperlé Ouest or Kergostiou, Quimperlé Centre, Clohars Carnoët exit and follow D16 to Clohars Carnoët. Then take D24 for Le Pouldu and follow site signs in village.

GPS: 47.76867, -3.54508

Charges guide

Per unit incl. 2 persons and electricity	€ 16,50 - € 39,50
extra person	€ 4,00 - € 6,50
child (under 7 yrs)	€ 2,85 - € 4,00
dog	€ 2,80

France – Le Pouldu

Camping les Embruns

2 rue du Philosophe Alain, le Pouldu Plages, F-29360 Clohars-Carnoët (Finistère)
t: 02 98 39 91 07   e: camping-les-embruns@orange.fr
alanrogers.com/FR29180   www.camping-les-embruns.com

Accommodation: ☑ Pitch   ☑ Mobile home/chalet   ○ Hotel/B&B   ○ Apartment

This site is unusual in that it is located in the heart of a village, yet is only 250 metres from a sandy cove. The entrance with its code operated barrier and wonderful floral displays, is the first indication that this is a well tended and well organised site, and the owners have won numerous regional and national awards for its superb presentation. The 176 pitches (100 occupied by mobile homes) are separated by trees, shrubs and bushes, and most have electricity (16A Europlug), water and drainage. There is a covered, heated swimming pool, a circular paddling pool and a water play pool and slide. A recent addition is the wellness centre with sauna and massage facilities. It is only a short walk to the village centre with all its attractions and services. It is also close to beautiful countryside and the Carnoët Forest which are good for walking and cycling.

You might like to know

Le Pouldu has three superb, sandy, south-facing beaches with good water quality, one just 250 m. from the campsite. There are numerous creeks, moorings, watersports opportunities, and sea and lake fishing.

○ Beach on site
☑ Beach within 1 km
☑ Sandy beach
☑ Blue Flag quality
☑ Lifeguard *(high season)*
○ Sun lounger and/or deckchair hire
☑ Watersports *(e.g. sailing or windsurfing)*
☑ Snacks and drinks
○ Sunshades/sunbeds
○ Dogs allowed *(on the beach)*

France – La Forêt-Fouesnant

Camping de Kéranterec

Route de Port la Forêt, F-29940 La Forêt-Fouesnant (Finistère)
t: 02 98 56 98 11 e: info@camping-keranterec.com
alanrogers.com/FR29240 www.camping-keranterec.com

Accommodation: ☑ Pitch ☑ Mobile home/chalet ○ Hotel/B&B ○ Apartment

Facilities: Two modern, fully equipped toilet blocks kept very clean include washbasins in cubicles, baby baths and facilities for disabled visitors. Laundry facilities. Small shop and bar (24/5-6/9) and takeaway (July/Aug). TV room with satellite. Heated outdoor swimming pool (1/5-10/9) with paddling pool, jacuzzi and three slides and a covered, heated pool (19/4-10/9). Tennis. Boules. Play area. In July/Aug organised events and activities for all the family, and a free children's club. Free WiFi. Off site: Attractive sandy beach of Kerleven 10 minutes walk. Golf 800 m. Riding 2 km.

Open: 12 April - 20 September.

Directions: From N165 take D70 Concarneau exit. At first roundabout take D44 (Fouesnant). After 2.5 km. turn right at T-junction, and follow for 2.5 km. and turn left (Port La Forêt). Go over roundabout, (Port La Forêt). After 1 km. turn left (site signed), then in 400 m. turn left to site.

GPS: 47.89923, -3.95505

Charges guide

Per unit incl. 2 persons and electricity	€ 16,00 - € 34,00
extra person	€ 7,00 - € 8,50
child (1-7 yrs)	€ 3,00 - € 4,00
dog	€ 2,00 - € 3,00

A well established family run site with a very French ambience, Kéranterec has 265 grassy pitches in two distinct areas. The upper part of the site is more open and has little shade, and is also largely taken up by private mobile homes. The lower and more mature area is predominantly for tourers, with terraced pitches set in a former orchard. Spacious and divided by mature hedging, all pitches have electrical connections (25 m. cable advised) and most also offer water and drainage. Some pitches have shade from the many trees on the lower part of the site, and some also overlook the little cove at the rear of the site. The trees still provide fruit for the cider produced on site (which we can highly recommend!). At the rear of the site a gate leads to a small beach and the coastal footpath to Concarneau (8 km). The area around La Forêt-Fouesnant is very much 'picture postcard' Brittany – plenty of enticing crêperies and seafood restaurants, enchanting medieval villages and towns and delightful hidden coves. For these and many other reasons, there are plenty of campsites to choose from and Camping de Kéranterec is well worth considering.

You might like to know

Walkers can take the coastal path and explore the many beaches and creeks in the area.

☑ Beach on site
☑ Beach within 1 km
☑ Sandy beach
○ Blue Flag quality
☑ Lifeguard (high season)
○ Sun lounger and/or deckchair hire
☑ Watersports (e.g. sailing or windsurfing)
○ Snacks and drinks
○ Sunshades/sunbeds
○ Dogs allowed (on the beach)

Facilities: The main toilet block provides British style toilets, showers, washing cubicles and good facilities for disabled visitors. A second block opens in high season. Washing machine and dryers. Shop, bar and terrace, with snacks (all July/Aug). Covered swimming pool (15/6-15/9). Play area. Games/TV room. Entertainment in July/Aug. Free WiFi in bar. Off site: Riding 500 m. Beach and fishing 1.5 km. Shops in Plomeur 3 km.

Open: 1 April - 31 October.

Directions: From Pont l'Abbé the D785 south to Plomeur, then follow signs for Pointe de La Torche. After 3 km. site is signed to left.

GPS: 47.832859, -4.326355

Charges guide

Per unit incl. 2 persons and electricity € 17,10 - € 23,40	
extra person € 3,50 - € 4,90	
child (0-7 yrs) € 2,20 - € 3,00	
dog no charge - € 2,00	

France – Plomeur-la Torche

Camping de la Torche

Pointe de la Roche, F-29120 Plomeur-la Torche (Finistère)
t: 02 98 58 62 82 e: info@campingdelatorche.fr
alanrogers.com/FR29370 www.campingdelatorche.fr

Accommodation: ☑ Pitch ☑ Mobile home/chalet ◯ Hotel/B&B ◯ Apartment

Probably a 'must stay' site for surfers, this rural, family owned, wooded campsite, like so many in this part of Brittany, comes to life in July and August. The natural beauty of the wide sandy beaches of la Torche can be accessed direct from the site via a footpath (1.5 km). La Torche is internationally renowned as a paradise for all boardsports, particularly windsurfing. The site has 155 pitches (99 for tourers), divided by trees and hedges and tending to the generous in size. Most have 6A electricity connections and 50 have water and drainage also. Around 56 chalets and mobile homes are discreetly positioned amongst the trees. After an energetic or a relaxing day on the beach, you can enjoy a drink at the bar or on the terrace overlooking the site's pool. There is one modern toilet block of a very good standard. Provisions are available at a supermarket in Plomeur (3 km).

You might like to know

There is a choice of surf schools nearby, including instruction for 5-8 year olds.

◯ Beach on site
◯ Beach within 1 km
☑ Sandy beach
◯ Blue Flag quality
◯ Lifeguard *(high season)*
◯ Sun lounger and/or deckchair hire
☑ Watersports *(e.g. sailing or windsurfing)*
◯ Snacks and drinks
◯ Sunshades/sunbeds
☑ Dogs allowed *(on the beach)*

Facilities: Very clean sanitary blocks include provision for disabled visitors. Washing machines. Motorcaravan services. Large supermarket, restaurant, takeaway, pizzeria and bar. Four outdoor pools with slides and flumes (20/5-10/9). Indoor pool (all season). Fitness room. Massage (Institut de Beauté). Tennis. Play areas. Miniclub, organised entertainment in season. Bicycle hire. WiFi throughout site (charged). ATM. Charcoal barbecues are not permitted. Hotel (12 rooms). Off site: Path to the beach 300 m. Fishing and riding. Golf 30 km.

Open: 13 May - 13 September.

Directions: Turn off D101 Hourtin-Soulac road 3 km. north of Hourtin. Then join D101E signed Hourtin-Plage. Site is 300 m. from the beach.

GPS: 45.22297, -1.16465

Charges guide

Per unit incl. 2 persons and electricity € 30,00 - € 58,00	
extra person € 5,00 - € 10,00	
child (3-9 yrs) € 4,00 - € 9,00	
dog € 3,00 - € 7,00	

France – Hourtin-Plage

Airotel Camping de la Côte d'Argent

F-33990 Hourtin-Plage (Gironde)
t: 05 56 09 10 25 e: info@cca33.com
alanrogers.com/FR33110 www.cca33.com

Accommodation: ☑ Pitch ☑ Mobile home/chalet ☑ Hotel/B&B ○ Apartment

Côte d'Argent is a large, well equipped site for leisurely family holidays. It makes an ideal base for walkers and cyclists with over 100 km. of cycle lanes in the area. Hourtin-Plage is a pleasant invigorating resort on the Atlantic coast and a popular location for watersports enthusiasts. The site's top attraction is its pool complex, where wooden bridges connect the pools and islands, and there are sunbathing and play areas plus an indoor heated pool. The site has 600 touring pitches (all with 10A electricity), not always clearly defined, arranged under trees with some on sand. High quality entertainment takes place at the impressive bar/restaurant near the entrance. Spread over 20 hectares of undulating sand-based terrain and in the midst of a pine forest, the site is well organised and ideal for children.

You might like to know

Majestic pine forests, tranquillity and the beauty of unspoiled nature are yours to enjoy at this Atlantic coast resort. The campsite entrance is just 300 m. from a vast expanse of fine sand.

○ Beach on site
☑ Beach within 1 km
☑ Sandy beach
○ Blue Flag quality
☑ Lifeguard *(high season)*
○ Sun lounger and/or deckchair hire
○ Watersports *(e.g. sailing or windsurfing)*
○ Snacks and drinks
○ Sunshades/sunbeds
○ Dogs allowed *(on the beach)*

Facilities: Seven modern blocks of individual design with good facilities including showers with washbasin and WC. Facilities for disabled visitors. Baby bathroom. Launderette. Motorcaravan services. Supermarket, bakery and newsagent. Other shops (2/6-14/9). ATM. Restaurants, bars and takeaway. Hairdresser. Balnéo spa (afternoons). Gym. Heated indoor pool. Outdoor pools (all season). Tennis courts. Multisports courts. Play areas. Trampolines. Children's clubs. Evening entertainment. Sporting activities. Bicycle hire. Bus to Sérignan village (July/Aug). Beach (lifeguards 15/6-15/9). WiFi over site (charged). Gas barbecues only. Off site: Fishing 1 km. Riding 1.5 km. Golf 15 km. Sailing and windsurfing school on beach. Local markets. Ferry to Valras Plage.

Open: 23 April - 28 September.

Directions: From A9 exit A75 (Béziers Centre) and exit 64 towards Sérignan, D64 (9 km). Before Sérignan, turn left, Sérignan-Plage (4 km). At small sign (blue) turn right. At T-junction turn left over small road bridge and after left hand bend. Site is 100 m.

GPS: 43.26308, 3.31976

Charges guide

Per unit incl. 2 persons and electricity	€ 19,00 - € 65,00
extra person	€ 6,00 - € 10,00
child (3-7 yrs)	no charge - € 9,00
dog	€ 5,00

Low season offers. Discounts in low season for children under 7 yrs.

France – Sérignan-Plage

Yelloh! Village le Sérignan-Plage

Le Sérignan Plage, F-34410 Sérignan-Plage (Hérault)
t: 04 67 32 35 33 e: info@leserignanplage.com
alanrogers.com/FR34070 www.leserignanplage.com

Accommodation: ☑ Pitch ☑ Mobile home/chalet ○ Hotel/B&B ○ Apartment

A lively and vibrant site with direct access onto a superb 600 m. sandy beach (including a naturist section), plus two swimming pool complexes and an indoor pool, this is a must for a Mediterranean holiday. It is a busy, friendly, family orientated site with a very comprehensive range of amenities and activities for children. There are now over 1,200 pitches with 260 for touring units. They are fairly level, on sandy soil and all have 10A electricity. The collection of spa pools (balnéo) built in Romanesque style with colourful terracing and columns is overlooked by a very smart restaurant, Le Villa, available to use in the afternoons (used by the adjacent naturist site in the mornings). The owners, Jean-Guy and Catherine, continually surprise us with their flair and unique style in developing and organising the site. Their latest project is a shallow fun pool with colourful play equipment. There are over 300 mobile homes and chalets to let, plus some 400 privately owned units and a good number of tour operator pitches. There is a range of sporting activities, children's clubs and evening entertainment – a good holiday choice with something for all.

You might like to know

Yelloh! Village Le Serignan Plage has a brilliant swimming pool complex with a new aquatic play area for children, a lagoon style pool covering 850 sq.m, and a covered pool for very young swimmers.

- ☑ Beach on site
- ○ Beach within 1 km
- ☑ Sandy beach
- ☑ Blue Flag quality
- ☑ Lifeguard *(high season)*
- ☑ Sun lounger and/or deckchair hire
- ☑ Watersports *(e.g. sailing or windsurfing)*
- ☑ Snacks and drinks
- ☑ Sunshades/sunbeds
- ○ Dogs allowed *(on the beach)*

Facilities:
Good, modern toilet blocks include baby rooms, children's toilets, facilities for disabled visitors (whole site wheelchair friendly). En-suite facilities on payment. Washing machines and dryers. Motorcaravan services. Fridge hire. Large well stocked shop. Bar, restaurant and takeaway. Swimming pool complex (lifeguards all season). Good play area. Miniclub (4-8 yrs). Boules. New gym with sauna, games room, beauty salon and massage. Multisports court. Bicycle hire. Games/TV room. Variety of evening entertainment. WiFi throughout (charged). Communal barbecue (only gas and electric permitted on pitches). Off site: Fishing and riding 1 km. Portiragnes-Plage with beach bars and restaurants 2 km. Golf 10 km.

Open: 31 May - 6 September.

Directions: From A9 exit 35 (Béziers Est) take N112 south towards Sérignan (1 km). Large roundabout follow signs for Cap d'Agde, watch carefully for D37, Portiragnes (1-2 km), follow signs for Portiragnes-Plage. Site well signed before Portiragnes-Plage (5 km).

GPS: 43.29153, 3.37348

Charges guide

Per unit incl. 2 persons and electricity	€ 21,00 - € 44,00
extra person	€ 5,00 - € 10,00
child (under 4 yrs)	no charge - € 5,00
dog	€ 2,00 - € 6,00
private sanitary unit	€ 8,50 - € 11,00

France – Portiragnes-Plage

Camping Caravaning les Mimosas

Port Cassafières, F-34420 Portiragnes-Plage (Hérault)
t: 04 67 90 92 92   e: les.mimosas.portiragnes@wanadoo.fr
alanrogers.com/FR34170   www.mimosas.com

Accommodation: ☑ Pitch   ☑ Mobile home/chalet   ○ Hotel/B&B   ○ Apartment

Les Mimosas is quite a large site with 400 pitches – 200 for touring units, the remainder for mobile homes – in a rural situation. The level, grassy pitches are of average size, separated and numbered in regular avenues, all with 6A electricity (long leads may be required), some have good shade, others have less. The pool area, a real feature of the site, includes a most impressive wave pool, various toboggans, the 'Space Hole' water slide, a large swimming pool and a super paddling pool (nine pools in all) with lots of free sun beds. This is a friendly, family run site with families in mind, with something new for each year. Les Mimosas has a less hectic situation than sites closer to the beach. However, it is possible to walk to a lovely sandy beach. There is lots going on and many day trips and excursions are arranged all season, from canoeing to visiting castles. Portiragnes-Plage is about 2 km. away and can be reached by cycle tracks. The Canal du Midi runs along the edge of the site (no access), providing another easy cycle route.

You might like to know

Ideally situated on the Canal du Midi, just 1 km. from a small, sandy beach. Portiragnes Plage (2 km) has pedalo hire and watersports, including water skiing and wake boarding.

○ Beach on site
☑ Beach within 1 km
☑ Sandy beach
○ Blue Flag quality
○ Lifeguard *(high season)*
○ Sun lounger and/or deckchair hire
○ Watersports *(e.g. sailing or windsurfing)*
☑ Snacks and drinks
☑ Sunshades/sunbeds
☑ Dogs allowed *(on the beach)*

Facilities: Good toilet facilities are centrally located and include some washbasins in private cabins, a baby room and en-suite facilities for disabled visitors. Motorcaravan services. Newly developed fitness and sports area near the beach. In high season beach games, dances, sangria evenings etc, are organised, all aimed particularly towards families along with a small bar/snack bar (high season). Only gas barbecues on pitches. Communal barbecues area. WiFi throughout (charged). Off site: Local market day Tuesday. Bicycle hire and fishing 100 m. Riding 1 km. Boat launching 1.5 km. Golf 2 km. Aqua park at Agde 5 km.

Open: 1 April - 11 October.

Directions: From A9 exit 34 take N312 towards Agde, then N112 towards Sète keeping a look-out for signs to Marseillan-Plage off this road. Site is well signed in Marseillan-Plage.

GPS: 43.3206, 3.5501

Charges guide

Per unit incl. 2 persons and electricity	€ 16,30 - € 33,50
extra person (over 2 yrs)	€ 3,00 - € 6,00
dog	€ 2,00 - € 3,00

France – Marseillan-Plage

Camping la Créole

74 avenue des Campings, F-34340 Marseillan-Plage (Hérault)
t: 04 67 21 92 69 e: campinglacreole@orange.fr
alanrogers.com/FR34220 www.campinglacreole.com

Accommodation: ☑ Pitch ☑ Mobile home/chalet ○ Hotel/B&B ○ Apartment

This is a surprisingly tranquil, well cared for small campsite in the middle of this bustling resort and will appeal to those seeking a rather less frenetic ambience typical of many sites in this area. The Chaput family, who run the site, originally worked the land as a vineyard but developed it into a campsite in 1973. It offers 100 good sized, level, sandy pitches, all with 6A electricity and mostly with shade from mature trees and shrubs. There are also 18 mobile homes available to rent. It benefits from direct access to an extensive sandy beach (secure gated access) and the fact that there is no swimming pool actually contributes to the tranquillity. The beach will be the main attraction here no doubt, and the town's extensive range of bars, restaurants and shops are all within a couple of minutes walk. It is well situated for visiting Sète, a miniature Venice, or Pézenas with an interesting history and lots of art and craft shops. Cap d'Agde, a modern resort with its large marina and super water park for children is popular. If you take a trip on the famous Canal du Midi you may get to see the oyster beds in the Etang de Thau, the inland saltwater lake.

You might like to know

Children can swim safely on the gently sloping beach with its fine sand. There is plenty of shade on the campsite, and all shops and services are within 100 m.

- ☑ Beach on site
- ○ Beach within 1 km
- ☑ Sandy beach
- ☑ Blue Flag quality
- ☑ Lifeguard *(high season)*
- ○ Sun lounger and/or deckchair hire
- ☑ Watersports *(e.g. sailing or windsurfing)*
- ☑ Snacks and drinks
- ○ Sunshades/sunbeds
- ☑ Dogs allowed *(on the beach)*

France – Portiragnes-Plage

Camping les Sablons

Avenue des Muriers, F-34420 Portiragnes-Plage (Hérault)
t: 04 67 90 90 55 e: contact@les-sablons.com
alanrogers.com/FR34400 www.les-sablons.com

Accommodation: ☑ Pitch ☑ Mobile home/chalet ○ Hotel/B&B ○ Apartment

Facilities: Well equipped, modernised toilet blocks include large showers, some with washbasins. Baby baths and facilities for disabled visitors. Supermarket, bakery and newsagent. Restaurant, bar and takeaway. Swimming pool complex. Entertainment and activity programme with sports, music and cultural activities. Children's club. Beach club. Tennis. Archery. Play areas. Bicycle hire. Electronic games. ATM. Internet access. WiFi throughout (charged). Off site: Village and bicycle hire 100 m. Beach and riding 200 m. Canal du Midi 1 km. Parc Adventure (high wire adventure park) 1.5 km.

Open: April - September.

Directions: From A9 exit 35 (Béziers Est) follow signs for Vias and Agde (N112). After large roundabout pass exit to Cers then take exit for Portiragnes (D37). Follow for 5 km. and pass over Canal du Midi towards Portiragnes-Plage. Site is on left after roundabout.
GPS: 43.28003, 3.36396

Charges guide

Per unit incl. 2 persons and electricity	€ 20,00 - € 52,00
extra person	€ 6,00 - € 10,00
child (under 13 yrs, acc. to age)	no charge - € 10,00
dog	€ 4,00

Les Sablons is an impressive and popular site with 680 pitches and lots going on, a village in itself. Most of the facilities are arranged around the entrance with shops, a restaurant, a bar and a large pool complex with no less than five slides and three heated pools. There is also direct access to a white sandy beach at the back of the site, close to a small lake. There is good shade on the majority of the site, although some of the newer touring pitches have less shade but are nearer the gate to the beach. On level sandy grass, all 220 touring pitches have 6A electricity. The remainder are taken by a range of mobile homes and chalets (many for hire, and a few for use by tour operators). A new entertainment office enables you to book a wide range of sporting, cultural and musical activities as well as excursions. Children's clubs, daily activities and evening entertainment are organised. In fact, this is a real holiday venue aiming to keep all the family happy. Some visitors simply stay on the site for their entire holiday – it certainly has everything. The site is very convenient for Béziers airport.

You might like to know

The site has direct access to the beach and dunes (closed 23.00-07.00). There is also a lake with hides for birdwatching.

☑ Beach on site
○ Beach within 1 km
☑ Sandy beach
○ Blue Flag quality
☑ Lifeguard *(high season)*
○ Sun lounger and/or deckchair hire
☑ Watersports *(e.g. sailing or windsurfing)*
☑ Snacks and drinks
○ Sunshades/sunbeds
○ Dogs allowed *(on the beach)*

Camping le Méditerranée Plage

Côte Ouest, F-34450 Vias (Hérault)
t: 04 67 90 99 07   e: contact@mediterranee-plage.com
alanrogers.com/FR34410   www.mediterranee-plage.com

Accommodation: ☑ Pitch ☑ Mobile home/chalet ○ Hotel/B&B ○ Apartment

Facilities: Two large toilet blocks are modern, one very impressive with a special smart nursery unit. Two small ones are more traditional. Facilities for disabled visitors. Laundry. Motorcaravan services. Supermarket. Smart restaurant (facing stage for entertainment) and bar. Snack bar. Hairdressers. TV room. Play area. Games room. Multisports court. Tennis. Archery. Windsurfing possible from beach. Bicycle hire. Activity programme, children's entertainment, circus school, evening shows and dancing. WiFi (charged). Off site: Riding and fishing 2 km. Golf 15 km. Canal du Midi nearby. Luna Park at Vias. Local markets in Vias (Wed and Sat am), Agde (Thurs. am) and Beziers (Fri. am).

Open: 31 March - 30 September.

Directions: From A9 exit 35 (Béziers Est) follow directions for Agde and Sète on N112. After 4.2 km. turn for Portiragnes. Pass village and continue for 2.5 km. over Canal du Midi then turn left and follow site signs.

GPS: 43.28202, 3.37105

Charges guide

Per unit incl. 2 persons and electricity	€ 16,90 - € 43,80
extra person	€ 3,30 - € 8,10
child (2-10 yrs)	€ 2,20 - € 6,20
dog	€ 1,00 - € 4,10

Set beside the beach in a quiet part of the coast, this site is somewhat different from the majority of beach sites. It has a most impressive entertainment complex situated to one side of the site with very comfortable outdoor seating facing a large stage for entertainment and a very smart bar and restaurant. The colourful furnishings and modern design reflect its Mediterranean setting. The site is very well cared for, with 410 pitches (some 185 used for touring units). Either grassy with a degree of shade or, as you get nearer the beach, more sandy with less shade, all have 6A electricity. The site's other claim to being different is its circus workshop weeks for children (6-12 years) designed to introduce them to the magical world of circus and culminating in a performance for parents each Friday. A new half-board 'country week' includes a dancing course. The pool area and shops – including a bakery and snack bar – are near the entrance which is busy during the day. The site and the white sandy beach are very popular with Dutch and German visitors.

You might like to know

As a change from the beach, a cycle route runs along the Canal du Midi to Béziers, with its 13th-century cathedral.

- ☑ Beach on site
- ○ Beach within 1 km
- ☑ Sandy beach
- ○ Blue Flag quality
- ○ Lifeguard *(high season)*
- ○ Sun lounger and/or deckchair hire
- ○ Watersports *(e.g. sailing or windsurfing)*
- ☑ Snacks and drinks
- ○ Sunshades/sunbeds
- ☑ Dogs allowed *(on the beach)*

Facilities: Four toilet blocks, one heated. One block with fun facilities for children based on Disney characters. Facilities for disabled guests. Laundry facilities. Motorcaravan services. Shops, bar/restaurant, takeaway (16/4-7/9; limited hours until June). Swimming pool complex with three pools (all season). Spa, fitness centre and sauna. Play area. Games room. Sports areas. Boules. Tennis. Bicycle hire. Minigolf. Fishing. Riding. Sailing school (15/6-15/9). Communal barbecues. WiFi (charged). Free bus to beach (July/Aug). Off site: Walking and cycle ways in the forest. Shops in Léon 4 km. Atlantic beaches 5 km. Golf 10 km.

Open: 12 April - 21 September.

Directions: Site is off D652 Mimizan-Léon road, 4 km. south of crossroads with D42 at St Girons. The road to the lake and the site is signed at Vielle.

GPS: 43.90285, -1.3125

Charges guide

Per unit incl. 2 persons and electricity (10A)	€ 17,20 - € 51,10
extra person	€ 2,30 - € 7,20
child (3-12 yrs)	€ 1,70 - € 6,20
dog	€ 1,30 - € 4,90

France – Vielle-Saint-Girons

Sunêlia le Col-Vert

Lac de Léon, 1548 route de l'Etang, F-40560 Vielle-Saint-Girons (Landes)
t: 08 90 71 00 01 e: contact@colvert.com
alanrogers.com/FR40050 www.colvert.com

Accommodation: ☑ Pitch ☑ Mobile home/chalet ○ Hotel/B&B ○ Apartment

This large, well maintained campsite is well laid out on the shores of Lac de Léon and offers 380 touring pitches and 350 mobile homes for rent. The pitches range from simple ones to those with water and a drain, and there are eight with private, well designed, modern sanitary facilities. In low season it is a quiet site and those pitches beside the lake offer a wonderful backdrop to relaxing pastimes. During the main season it is a lively place for children of all ages. A pool complex offers a standard pool for swimming, a pool for children with a water canon and fountains, plenty of sunbeds and a heated indoor pool. Swimming is also permitted in the lake alongside the many water-based activities. A fitness and beauty spa offers a wide range of treatments. This extensive but natural site edges a nature reserve and stretches along the Lac de Léon, a conservation area, for 1 km. on a narrow frontage. This makes it particularly suitable for those who want to practise watersports such as sailing and windsurfing, there is also a water playground with inflatable games. An overall charge is made for some but not all of the leisure activities.

You might like to know

Bordering the Lac de Léon and at the heart of a vast nature reserve, le Col-Vert was the first French campsite to receive the Ecolabel award. The fine sandy beaches of the Côte d'Argent are nearby.

○ Beach on site

○ Beach within 1 km

☑ Sandy beach

☑ Blue Flag quality

☑ Lifeguard *(high season)*

○ Sun lounger and/or deckchair hire

☑ Watersports *(e.g. sailing or windsurfing)*

☑ Snacks and drinks

○ Sunshades/sunbeds

☑ Dogs allowed *(on the beach)*

Camping Club International Eurosol

Route de la Plage, F-40560 Saint Girons-Plage (Landes)
t: 05 58 47 90 14   e: contact@camping-eurosol.com
alanrogers.com/FR40060   **www.camping-eurosol.com**

Accommodation: ☑ Pitch   ☑ Mobile home/chalet   ○ Hotel/B&B   ○ Apartment

Privately owned, Eurosol is an attractive, friendly and well maintained site extending over 15 hectares of undulating ground amongst mature pine trees giving good shade. Of the 356 touring pitches, 231 have electricity (10A) with 120 fully serviced. A wide range of mobile homes and chalets, which are being updated, are available for rent. This is very much a family site with multi-lingual entertainers. Many games and tournaments are organised and a beach volleyball competition is held regularly in front of the bar. The adjacent boules terrain is floodlit. An excellent sandy beach 700 metres from the site has supervised bathing in high season and is ideal for surfing. The landscaped swimming pool complex is impressive with three large pools, one of which is covered and heated, and a large children's paddling pool. There is a convivial restaurant and takeaway food service. A large supermarket is well stocked with fresh bread daily and international newspapers. A number of cycle trails lead from the site through the vast forests of Les Landes, and a riding centre is located just 500 m. from Eurosol.

You might like to know

A quiet, very high quality camping village in the shade of the pine forest, and a great spot for unforgettable family holidays.

○ Beach on site
☑ Beach within 1 km
☑ Sandy beach
○ Blue Flag quality
☑ Lifeguard *(high season)*
○ Sun lounger and/or deckchair hire
○ Watersports *(e.g. sailing or windsurfing)*
☑ Snacks and drinks
☑ Sunshades/sunbeds
☑ Dogs allowed *(on the beach)*

Facilities: Four main toilet blocks and two smaller blocks are comfortable and clean with facilities for babies and disabled visitors. Motorcaravan services. Fridge rental. Well stocked shop and bar (all season). Restaurant, takeaway (1/6-7/9). Stage for live shows arranged in July/Aug. Outdoor swimming pool, paddling pool (all season) and heated, covered pool (May-July). Tennis. Multisports court. Bicycle hire. WiFi (charged). Charcoal barbecues are not permitted. Off site: Riding (July/Aug) 500 m. Surf school 500 m. Beach and fishing 700 m. Golf 18 km.

Open: 12 May - 13 September.

Directions: Turn off D652 at St Girons on D42 towards St Girons-Plage. Site is on left before coming to beach (4.5 km).

GPS: 43.95166, -1.35212

Charges guide

Per unit incl. 2 persons
and electricity € 20,00 - € 39,00

extra person (over 5 yrs) € 6,00

dog € 4,00

Facilities: Five toilet blocks (opened as required) are well maintained with showers and many washbasins in cabins. Facilities for babies, children and disabled visitors. Laundry facilities. Motorcaravan services. Fridge hire. Shop (freshly baked bread) and bar. Restaurant, snack bar, pizzas and takeaway. Covered pool and outdoor pools. Minigolf. Tennis. Bicycle hire. Play area. Entertainment and activities (high season). Gas or electric barbecues only. WiFi throughout (charged). Off site: Beach and fishing 500 m. Bus service and riding 1 km. Golf 8 km. Mimizan 8 km.

Open: 25 April - 19 September.

Directions: Heading west from Mimizan centre, take D626 passing Abbey Museum. Straight on at lights (crossing D87/D67), at next lights turn left. After 2 km. at T-junction turn left. Follow signs to site.
GPS: 44.20447, -1.29099

Charges guide

Per unit incl. 3 persons and electricity	€ 21,00 - € 57,00
extra person	€ 5,00 - € 10,00
child (3-12 yrs)	€ 4,00 - € 8,00
dog	€ 3,00 - € 6,00

France – Mimizan-Plage

Airotel Club Marina-Landes

Rue Marina, F-40200 Mimizan (Landes)
t: 05 58 09 12 66 e: contact@clubmarina.com
alanrogers.com/FR40080 www.marinalandes.com

Accommodation: ☑ Pitch ☑ Mobile home/chalet ○ Hotel/B&B ☑ Apartment

Well maintained and clean, with helpful staff, Club Marina-Landes would be a very good choice for a family holiday. Activities include discos, play groups for children, specially trained staff to entertain teenagers and concerts for more mature campers. There are numerous sports opportunities and a superb sandy beach nearby. The site has 356 touring pitches (316 with 10A electricity) and 147 mobile homes and chalets for rent. The pitches are on firm grass, most with hedges and they are large (mostly 100 sq.m. or larger). A nightly curfew ensures that all have a good night's sleep. A new leisure pool is planned. If ever a campsite could be said to have two separate identities, then Club Marina-Landes is surely the one. In early and late season it is quiet, with the pace of life in low gear – come July and until 1 September, all the facilities are open and there is fun for all the family with the chance that family members will only meet together at meal times.

You might like to know

Why not take the Mailloueyre lake trail (1 km, 15 minutes on foot)? The area is officially classified as a nature reserve and is a delight for botanists and nature lovers alike.

○ Beach on site
☑ Beach within 1 km
☑ Sandy beach
○ Blue Flag quality
☑ Lifeguard *(high season)*
○ Sun lounger and/or deckchair hire
☑ Watersports *(e.g. sailing or windsurfing)*
☑ Snacks and drinks
☑ Sunshades/sunbeds
☑ Dogs allowed *(on the beach)*

Facilities:
Facilities: Three good clean toilet blocks have washbasins in cabins and mainly British style toilets. Facilities for disabled visitors. Baby baths. Motorcaravan services. Shop with gas. New bar/restaurant complex with entertainment. Swimming pool complex (supervised July/Aug) with aquapark for children. Games room. Play area. Tennis. Bicycle hire. Boules. Archery. Fishing. Water skiing. Watersports equipment hire. Tournaments (June-Aug). Skateboard park. Trampolines. Miniclub. No charcoal barbecues on pitches. Communal barbecue areas. WiFi throughout (charged). Off site: Riding 3 km. Golf 8 km. Beach 18 km.

Open: 11 April - 30 August.

Directions: Take D652 from Sanguinet to Biscarrosse and site is signed on the right in 6 km. Turn right and follow tarmac road for 2 km.

GPS: 44.46052, -1.13065

Charges guide

Per unit incl. 2 persons and electricity	€ 27,50 - € 54,00
extra person	€ 5,30 - € 10,60
child (3-7 yrs)	€ 3,80 - € 8,70
dog	€ 6,20 - € 11,30

No credit cards.

France – Biscarrosse

Camping Resort la Rive

Route de Bordeaux, F-40600 Biscarrosse (Landes)
t: 05 58 78 12 33 e: info@larive.fr
alanrogers.com/FR40100 www.larive.fr

Accommodation: ☑ Pitch ☑ Mobile home/chalet ○ Hotel/B&B ○ Apartment

Surrounded by pine woods, la Rive has a superb beach-side location on Lac de Sanguinet. With a total of 800 pitches, it provides 250 mostly level, numbered and clearly defined touring pitches of 100 sq.m. all with electricity connections (10A). The swimming pool complex is wonderful with pools linked by water channels and bridges. There is also a jacuzzi, paddling pool and two large swimming pools all surrounded by sunbathing areas and decorated with palm trees. An indoor pool is heated and open all season. This is a friendly site with a good mix of nationalities. The latest additions are a super children's aquapark with various games, and a top quality bar/restaurant complex where regular entertainment is organised. There are plans to extend the outdoor pools with the addition of new slides more than 200 m. long. The beach is excellent, shelving gently to provide safe bathing for all ages. There are windsurfers and small craft can be launched from the site's slipway.

You might like to know

The fine sandy beach can be accessed from the campsite, and there is a wide range of watersports for the whole family.

- ☑ Beach on site
- ○ Beach within 1 km
- ☑ Sandy beach
- ○ Blue Flag quality
- ○ Lifeguard *(high season)*
- ○ Sun lounger and/or deckchair hire
- ☑ Watersports *(e.g. sailing or windsurfing)*
- ○ Snacks and drinks
- ○ Sunshades/sunbeds
- ○ Dogs allowed *(on the beach)*

Facilities: Nine well appointed, recently renovated toilet blocks with facilities for children and disabled visitors. Motorcaravan services. Good supermarket and various smaller shops in high season. Several restaurants, takeaway and three bars (all open all season). Large pool complex (no Bermuda shorts; open all season) including new covered pool and Polynesian themed bar. Tennis. Multisports pitch. Minigolf. Outdoor fitness area. Fishing. Bicycle hire. Riding centre. Organised activities including frequent discos and karaoke evenings (1/4-12/9). Spa, massages and beauty area. Only communal barbecues are allowed. WiFi over site (charged). Off site: Beach 400 m. Sailing 2 km. Golf 8 km.

Open: 1 April - 28 September.

Directions: Leave RN10 at Magescq exit heading for Soustons. Pass through Soustons following signs for Vieux-Boucau. Bypass this town and site is clearly signed to the left at second roundabout.

GPS: 43.79778, -1.40111

Charges guide

Per unit incl. 2 persons and electricity € 21,55 - € 61,80
extra person € 4,85 - € 9,10
child (under 13 yrs) € 3,85 - € 6,25
dog € 3,10 - € 5,85

Airotel le Vieux Port

Plage Sud, F-40660 Messanges (Landes)
t: 01 76 76 70 00 e: contact@levieuxport.com
alanrogers.com/**FR40180** www.levieuxport.com

Accommodation: ☑ Pitch ☑ Mobile home/chalet ○ Hotel/B&B ○ Apartment

A well established destination appealing particularly to families with teenage children, this lively site has 1,546 pitches (975 for touring) of mixed sizes, most with electricity (6A). The camping area is well shaded by pines and pitches are generally of a good size, attractively grouped around the toilet blocks. There are many tour operators here and well over a third of the site is taken up with mobile homes and chalets. An enormous 7,000 sq.m. aquatic park is now open, and is the largest on any French campsite. This heated complex is exceptional, boasting five outdoor pools (all 25°C), three large water slides plus waves and a heated spa. There is also a heated indoor pool. The area to the north of Bayonne is heavily forested and a number of very large campsites are attractively located close to the superb Atlantic beaches. Le Vieux Port is probably the largest, and certainly one of the most impressive, of these. At the back of the site a path leads across the dunes to a good beach (400 m). Other recent innovations include an outdoor fitness area and a superb riding centre. All in all, this is a lively site with a great deal to offer an active family.

You might like to know

The whole family will love the enormous sandy beach, just five minutes away and accessed directly from the site.

○ Beach on site
☑ Beach within 1 km
☑ Sandy beach
○ Blue Flag quality
☑ Lifeguard *(high season)*
○ Sun lounger and/or deckchair hire
☑ Watersports *(e.g. sailing or windsurfing)*
☑ Snacks and drinks
○ Sunshades/sunbeds
○ Dogs allowed *(on the beach)*

Facilities: Seven toilet blocks of a high standard and very well maintained, have washbasins in cabins, large showers, baby rooms and facilities for disabled visitors. Motorcaravan services. Washing machines and dryers. Fridge rental. Supermarket. Bars, restaurants and takeaways. Indoor pool, jacuzzi and sauna (charged July/Aug). Outdoor pool area with jacuzzi and paddling pool (15/6-15/9). Multisports pitch. Play area. Bicycle hire. Beach access. WiFi throughout (charged). Off site: Fishing and beach 300 m. Golf and tennis 700 m. Sailing 6 km. Riding 8 km.

Open: Easter - 1 November.

Directions: From the N10 take D142 to Lèon, then D652 to Moliets-et-Mar. Follow signs to Moliets-Plage, site is well signed.

GPS: 43.85242, -1.38732

Charges guide

Per unit incl. 2 persons and electricity	€ 22,70 - € 50,00
extra person	€ 6,00 - € 8,90
child (under 13 yrs)	€ 4,00 - € 6,30
dog no charge	- € 5,30

Prices are for reserved pitches.

France – Moliets-Plage

Le Camping Saint-Martin

Avenue de l'Océan, F-40660 Moliets-Plage (Landes)
t: 05 58 48 52 30 e: contact@camping-saint-martin.fr
alanrogers.com/FR40190 www.camping-saint-martin.fr

Accommodation: ☑ Pitch ☑ Mobile home/chalet ○ Hotel/B&B ○ Apartment

A family site aimed mainly at couples and young families, le Saint-Martin offers 383 touring pitches and 173 mobile homes and chalets available for rent. First impressions are of a neat, tidy, well cared for site and the direct access to a wonderful fine sandy beach is an added bonus. The pitches are mainly typically French in style with low hedges separating them, and with some shade. Electricity hook ups are 10/15A and a number of pitches also have water and drainage. Entertainment in high season is low key (with the emphasis on quiet nights) – daytime competitions and a miniclub, plus the occasional evening entertainment, well away from the pitches and with no discos or karaoke. With a top class pool complex and an 18-hole golf course 700 m. away (special rates negotiated), this would be an ideal destination for a golfing weekend or longer stay.

You might like to know

Courant d'Huchet, a conservation area, is delightful and has a number of walks and some beautiful views.

☑ Beach on site
○ Beach within 1 km
☑ Sandy beach
○ Blue Flag quality
☑ Lifeguard *(high season)*
○ Sun lounger and/or deckchair hire
○ Watersports *(e.g. sailing or windsurfing)*
○ Snacks and drinks
○ Sunshades/sunbeds
☑ Dogs allowed *(on the beach)*

France – Biscarrosse

Camping Mayotte Vacances

368 chemin des Roseaux, F-40600 Biscarrosse (Landes)
t: 05 58 78 00 00 e: camping@mayottevacances.com
alanrogers.com/**FR40240** www.mayottevacances.com

Accommodation: ☑ Pitch ☑ Mobile home/chalet ○ Hotel/B&B ○ Apartment

This appealing site is set amongst pine trees on the edge of Lac de Biscarrosse. Drive down a tree- and flower-lined avenue and proceed toward the lake to shady, good sized pitches which blend well with the many tidy mobile homes that share the area. Divided by hedges, all 140 touring pitches have electricity (16A) and water taps. There may be some aircraft noise at times from a nearby army base. The pool complex is impressive, with various pools, slides, chutes, jacuzzi and sauna, all surrounded by paved sunbathing areas. The excellent lakeside beach provides safe bathing for all ages with plenty of watersports available. A comfortable restaurant and bar overlook the pool. A new, fully equipped gym is available free of charge. Children of all ages are catered for with organised clubs, play and sports areas and a games room. This well managed, clean and friendly site with helpful multi-lingual staff in reception should appeal to all and the facilities are open all season.

You might like to know

A choice of beaches is within 10 km. with kite surfing, beach huts, organised beach parties and a sailing school.

☑ Beach on site
○ Beach within 1 km
☑ Sandy beach
○ Blue Flag quality
○ Lifeguard *(high season)*
○ Sun lounger and/or deckchair hire
☑ Watersports *(e.g. sailing or windsurfing)*
☑ Snacks and drinks
○ Sunshades/sunbeds
☑ Dogs allowed *(on the beach)*

Facilities: Four good quality, clean toilet blocks (one open early season). Good facilities for visitors with disabilities. Motorcaravan services. Laundry. Supermarket, bar, restaurant and takeaway (5/4-26/9). Boutique. Comprehensive rental shop (July/Aug). Heated indoor and outdoor swimming pools, supervised July/Aug. and weekends. Play area. Further children's area (extra cost) with trampolines, inflatables and a small train. Bicycle hire. Fishing. Watersports. Organised activities and entertainment (July/Aug). Clubs for toddlers and teenagers (July/Aug). TV room. Gas barbecues only. Hairdressers (seasonal). ATM. WiFi throughout (charged). Off site: Riding and golf 4 km. Town 2 km. with restaurants, shops and bars. Beach 10 km.

Open: 4 April - 26 September.

Directions: From the north on D652 turn right on D333 (Chemin de Goubern). Pass through Goubern and Mayotte village. Take next right (signed to site) into Chemin des Roseaux.
GPS: 44.43495, -1.15505

Charges guide

Per unit incl. 2 persons	€ 19,00 - € 53,00
extra person	€ 6,00 - € 9,50
child (3-7 yrs)	no charge - € 5,00
dog	€ 6,50

France – Les Pieux

Camping le Grand Large

F-50340 Les Pieux (Manche)
t: 02 33 52 40 75 e: info@legrandlarge.com
alanrogers.com/FR50060 www.legrandlarge.com

Accommodation: ☑ Pitch ☑ Mobile home/chalet ○ Hotel/B&B ○ Apartment

Le Grand Large is a well established, quality family site with direct access to a long sandy beach and within a 20 km. drive of Cherbourg. It is a neat and tidy site with 119 touring pitches divided and separated by hedging giving an orderly, well laid out and attractive appearance. Almost all have electricity (10A Europlug), water and drainage. There are 49 mobile homes for rent in three separate areas. The reception area is at the entrance (with a security barrier) and the forecourt is decorated with flower beds. To the rear of the site and laid out in the sandhills is an excellent play area. Not surprisingly the sandy beach is the big attraction. The length of units is restricted to eight metres to prevent any problems accessing pitches. Roads around the site are tarmac and many of the delightful plants and shrubs that you see bordering these carry name tags in four languages. The pleasant views from the site stretch across the bay to the tip of the Cherbourg peninsula. Every effort is made at le Grand Large to attract and cater for families with young children, so noisy entertainment is not an option.

Facilities: Two well maintained toilet blocks. The main one is modern and includes washbasins in cubicles and some family rooms. Some showers and WCs have access to the outside of the building. Provision for disabled visitors. Baby bathroom. Laundry area. Motorcaravan services. Shop for basics, bar (all season). Restaurant and takeaway (4/7-28/8). Heated swimming and paddling pools (indoor all season, outdoor 13/6-6/9). Play area. Tennis. Boules. Fishing. TV room. Some entertainment (July/Aug). WiFi over site (charged). Off site: Bicycle hire and riding 5 km. Golf 15 km. Two supermarkets in Les Pieux. Day trips by ferry to the Channel Islands (May-Sept) from nearby Diellete.

Open: 11 April - 20 September.

Directions: From Cherbourg port take N13 south for 2 km. Branch right on D650 (previously D904) signed Carteret. Continue for 18 km. to Les Pieux. Take D4 in town and turn left just after 'Super U' supermarket. Follow site signs via D117/517.

GPS: 49.49452, -1.84246

Charges guide

Per unit incl. 2 persons and electricity	€ 23,00 - € 40,00
extra person	€ 5,00 - € 8,70
child (3-10 yrs)	€ 3,50 - € 5,00

You might like to know

Le Grand Large Les Pieux is on a gently sloping sandy beach facing the Channel Islands, and just 20 minutes from Cherbourg. Visit Cité de la Mer or have a day out on Jersey or Guernsey.

☑ Beach on site
○ Beach within 1 km
☑ Sandy beach
☑ Blue Flag quality
○ Lifeguard *(high season)*
○ Sun lounger and/or deckchair hire
○ Watersports *(e.g. sailing or windsurfing)*
☑ Snacks and drinks
○ Sunshades/sunbeds
☑ Dogs allowed *(on the beach)*

Facilities: Toilet blocks (one heated) have free hot water, washbasins in cubicles, baby baths and facilities for children and disabled visitors. Laundry facilities. Swimming pool with water slides (08/05-20/09). Play areas including ball pool. Tennis. TV. Entertainment programme in high season for all ages. Bicycle hire. Canoe hire. Beach. Guided tours. Internet access and WiFi (charged). Communal barbecue areas (gas or electric only on pitches). Off site: Fishing 50 m. Shop with bakery. Bar, restaurant, crêperie, takeaway all 200 m. Sailing 1.5 km. Riding 3.5 km. Golf 13 km.

Open: 8 May - 20 September.

Directions: From N165 at Auray take D28 (La Trinité-sur-Mer). On through town following signs to Carnac-Plage on D186. Site signed off this road to the south. Take care to take road signed to Kervillen Plage where it forks. At seafront turn right. Site is 300 m. on right. The site is well signed.

GPS: 47.57563, -3.02890

Charges guide

Per unit incl. 2 persons and electricity (10A)	€ 23,20 - € 45,30
extra person	€ 6,20
child (2-17 yrs)	€ 3,00 - € 4,65
dog no charge	- € 1,40

Camping de la Plage

Plage de Kervillen, F-56470 La Trinité-sur-Mer (Morbihan)
t: 02 97 55 73 28 e: camping@camping-plage.com
alanrogers.com/FR56020 www.camping-plage.com

Accommodation: ☑ Pitch ☑ Mobile home/chalet ○ Hotel/B&B ○ Apartment

The Carnac and La Trinité area of Brittany is popular with British holidaymakers. Camping de la Plage is a well established site with direct access to the safe, sandy beach of Kervillen Plage. There are 195 grass pitches, some of which are used by tour operators and others occupied by mobile homes (available to rent), but many are available for touring. Pitches are all hedged and of a good size (100 sq.m) and have 6/10A electricity, water and drainage. The site has a slight slope and a few pitches reflect this. With narrow roads and sharp bends, La Plage may not be suitable for larger units. The shop, restaurant and bar, 200 m. along the coast, and overlooking Quiberon Bay, are used by local residents and provide excellent value. The restaurant and takeaway have extensive menus. A lively entertainment programme for all ages in high season makes this an attractive site for family holidays. La Trinité is a world famous yachting centre and is a delightful place for an evening stroll. It also hosts a colourful market on Tuesdays and Thursdays.

You might like to know

There is a choice of beaches along the coast, some where dogs are allowed, some where you can practise watersports.

- ☑ Beach on site
- ○ Beach within 1 km
- ☑ Sandy beach
- ○ Blue Flag quality
- ☑ Lifeguard *(high season)*
- ○ Sun lounger and/or deckchair hire
- ○ Watersports *(e.g. sailing or windsurfing)*
- ☑ Snacks and drinks
- ○ Sunshades/sunbeds
- ○ Dogs allowed *(on the beach)*

Camping Do Mi Si La Mi

31 rue de la Vierge, Saint Julien-Plage, F-56170 Quiberon (Morbihan)
t: 02 97 50 22 52   e: camping@domisilami.com
alanrogers.com/FR56360   www.domisilami.com

Accommodation: ☑ Pitch ☑ Mobile home/chalet ○ Hotel/B&B ○ Apartment

Occupying a five-hectare site on the Quiberon Peninsula, just 100 metres from the sandy beaches, this campsite has plenty to offer and is particularly quiet and laid back in low season. Of the 350 pitches, 189 are for touring and are set amongst high mature hedges and colourful shrubs giving plenty of shade and privacy; some have sea views. Long leads are required on a few pitches as the 10A electricty points can be shared between three or four pitches. The excellent amenities for children are in a well fenced area and include climbing frames, bouncy castles and multisports courts. Treasure hunts and other activities are organised daily in high season. The well managed reception is on the opposite side of the road to the campsite. This site is ideally situated for exploring this fascinating area.

You might like to know

Entertainment includes over 15 games, inflatables, multisports area, pétanque and table tennis. WiFi is available over the whole site.

○ Beach on site
☑ Beach within 1 km
☑ Sandy beach
○ Blue Flag quality
○ Lifeguard *(high season)*
○ Sun lounger and/or deckchair hire
○ Watersports *(e.g. sailing or windsurfing)*
☑ Snacks and drinks
○ Sunshades/sunbeds
○ Dogs allowed *(on the beach)*

Facilities: New, high quality sanitary block with hot showers. Facilities for disabled campers and young children. Separate laundry. Shop. Bar, restaurant and takeaway (1/4-15/9). TV room. Bouncy castles. Multisport courts. Bicycle hire. Children's club. WiFi throughout (charged). Off site: Bar, restaurant, supermarket 50 m. Beaches and bicycle hire 100 m. Town centre 2 km. Golf and riding 3 km.

Open: 1 April - 1 November.

Directions: From N165 Vannes-Lorient dual carriageway south of Auray, take Carnac/Ploemel exit. Continue southwest on D768 through the town of Plouharmel following signs for Quiberon. 25 km. from the N165 but before reaching Quiberon, the site is signed to the left at St Julien-Plage.
GPS: 47.49974, -3.12026

Charges guide

Per unit incl. 2 persons and electricity	€ 17,80 - € 27,80
extra person	€ 2,90 - € 5,00
child (under 7 yrs)	€ 2,10 - € 3,00
dog	€ 2,00 - € 2,50

Camping le Pavillon Royal

Avenue du Prince de Galles, F-64210 Bidart (Pyrénées-Atlantiques)
t: 05 59 23 00 54   e: info@pavillon-royal.com
alanrogers.com/FR64060   www.pavillon-royal.com

Accommodation: ☑ Pitch   ☑ Mobile home/chalet   ○ Hotel/B&B   ○ Apartment

Le Pavillon Royal has an excellent situation on raised ground overlooking the sea (100 m. from the beach), with good views along the coast to the south and to the north coast of Spain beyond. There is a large heated swimming pool and sunbathing area in the centre of the site. The camping area is divided up into 325 marked, level pitches, many of a good size. Seventy-five are reserved for tents and are only accessible on foot. The remainder are connected by asphalt roads. All have electricity. Much of the campsite is in full sun, although the area for tents is shaded. Beneath the site – and only a very short walk down – stretches a wide sandy beach where the Atlantic rollers provide ideal conditions for surfing. A central, marked out section of the beach is supervised by lifeguards (from mid June). There is also a section with rocks and pools. Reservation in high season is advisable.

You might like to know

The only campsite in the Basque country with direct access to the beach, where there is a surf school. The site also has a solar-heated swimming pool.

☑ Beach on site
☑ Beach within 1 km
☑ Sandy beach
○ Blue Flag quality
☑ Lifeguard *(high season)*
○ Sun lounger and/or deckchair hire
☑ Watersports *(e.g. sailing or windsurfing)*
☑ Snacks and drinks
☑ Sunshades/sunbeds
○ Dogs allowed *(on the beach)*

Facilities: Good quality toilet blocks with baby baths and two units for disabled visitors. Washing facilities (only two open at night). Washing machines, dryers. Motorcaravan services. Shop (including gas), restaurant and takeaway, bar, heated swimming and paddling pools, wellness facilities, fitness room (all open all season). Playground. General room, TV room, games room, films. Fishing. Surf school. Dogs are not accepted. WiFi throughout (charged). Off site: Golf 500 m. Bicycle hire 2 km. Riding 3 km. Sailing 5 km. New oceanographic centre at Biarritz.

Open: 15 May - 30 September.

Directions: From A63 exit 4, take the N10 south towards Bidart. At roundabout after the Intermarché supermarket turn right (signed for Biarritz). After 600 m. turn left at site sign.

GPS: 43.45458, -1.57649

Charges guide

Per unit incl. 2 persons, electricity and water	€ 33,00 - € 58,00
tent pitch	€ 27,00 - € 48,00
extra person (over 4 yrs)	€ 8,00 - € 14,00

France – Argelès-sur-Mer

MS Vacances Camping Club Le Littoral

Route du Littoral, F-66700 Argelès-sur-Mer (Pyrénées-Orientales)
t: 02 53 81 70 00   e: reservation@ms-vacances.com
alanrogers.com/FR66060   www.ms-vacances.com

Accommodation: ✔ Pitch   ✔ Mobile home/chalet   ○ Hotel/B&B   ○ Apartment

Facilities: Large modern toilet block, fully equipped and with some washbasins in cabins. Baby bath. Some facilities for disabled visitors. Washing machines. Shop, bar, restaurants and takeaway. Outdoor and covered heated swimming pools with slides. Solarium. Entertainment for all in high season. Only gas barbecues permitted. Play area. Fitness room. Bicycle hire. WiFi throughout (charged). Path to beach. Max. 1 dog per pitch. Free shuttle to beach (July-Aug). Off site: Tourist train in high season. Aquatic park, adventure park, karting, riding and minigolf all within walking distance.

Open: 11 April - 20 September.

Directions: From A9 take exit 43 (Le Boulou) and follow N114 for Argelès. At exit 10 follow directions for Taxo d'Avall then Plage Nord. Site is clearly signed off coast road in the St Cyprien direction.

GPS: 42.58066, 3.03324

Charges guide

Per unit incl. 2 persons and electricity	€ 25,00 - € 47,00
extra person	€ 6,20 - € 12,40
child no charge	- € 8,20

Le Littoral is only 800 metres from a fine, sandy beach via a footpath. The site offers plenty of accommodation in mobile homes as well as 25 good sized, level touring pitches with shade and 6A electricity. An attractive pool area is open all season. Argelès is a very popular holiday resort with good sandy beaches. A free shuttle bus runs to the beach and town centre in July and August. The border with Spain is only 30 km. away. The site has been taken over by MS Vacances and is looking smart with a new reception and tarmac roadways. It is well looked after and the pool area is particularly impressive, with indoor and outdoor pools, water slides and paddling pools. There is a lively activity and entertainment programme, with regular evening entertainment and clubs for teenagers and younger children.

You might like to know

Les Déferlantes music festival at Argelès-sur-Mer and the Fêtes de la Saint Vincent at Collioure are not to be missed, and the Abbey at Saint Martin du Canigou is worth the climb. 10%* discount for reservations made before 31 December 2104.
*Terms and conditions apply.

✔ Beach on site
✔ Beach within 1 km
✔ Sandy beach
✔ Blue Flag quality
✔ Lifeguard (high season)
○ Sun lounger and/or deckchair hire
✔ Watersports (e.g. sailing or windsurfing)
✔ Snacks and drinks
✔ Sunshades/sunbeds
✔ Dogs allowed (on the beach)

Facilities: Nine well equipped sanitary blocks are well placed around the site. Facilities for babies. Laundry. Motorcaravan services. Shops, bars, restaurant and takeaway. Swimming pools with lifeguards, jacuzzi and solarium. Fitness club. Children's clubs. Artistic workshops (pottery, crafts etc). Daily sports and entertainment programme. Day trips. Evening entertainment with cabaret. Disco. Communal barbecue. Sailing club. Beach club. Tennis. Bicycle hire. Play areas. WiFi throughout (charged). Direct access to beach.
Off site: Riding nearby. Rafting, canoeing and quad bike treks by arrangement. Canet 500 m. with tourist train in high season. Perpignan 10 km. Collioure, Port Vendres and the Spanish border.

Open: 26 April - 13 September.

Directions: Take exit 41 from A9 autoroute and follow signs for Canet. On outskirts of town follow signs for St Cyprien/Plage Sud. Site is very clearly signed on southern edge of Canet Plage.

GPS: 42.6757, 3.03135

Charges guide

Per unit incl. 2 persons and electricity	€ 24,20 - € 50,20
extra person	€ 8,00 - € 15,00
child (0-5 yrs)	no charge - € 7,50
dog	no charge - € 4,50

No credit cards.

France – Canet-en-Roussillon

Camping Mar Estang

Route de Saint Cyprien, F-66140 Canet-en-Roussillon (Pyrénées-Orientales)
t: 04 68 80 35 53   e: contactme@marestang.com
alanrogers.com/FR66090   www.marestang.com

Accommodation: ○ Pitch ◉ Mobile home/chalet ○ Hotel/B&B ○ Apartment

Le Mar Estang is a large, impressive, 'all singing, all dancing' site with something for everyone. Situated on the edge of Canet, between the Etang (part of the Réserve Naturelle de Canet/Saint Nazaire) and the sea, there is access to the sandy beach from the site by two tunnels under the road. If you don't fancy the beach, the site has not one but two attractive pool complexes linked by a bridge. They are amazing, providing slides, toboggans, jacuzzi, paddling pool and a heated pool, all with lifeguards. You can swim seriously, learn to swim or scuba dive or just enjoy the fun pools. Who needs the beach! There are 600 pitches in total, some 300 for touring units, with 6A electricity, and some degree of shade, on sandy ground. The rest are used by tour operators or have site-owned mobile homes to rent. A very wide range of activities and entertainment is organised all season, with children's clubs in high season and a beach club for watersports. Children and teenagers would have a great time here and parents would enjoy Canet-Plage with its esplanade, shops and restaurants.

You might like to know

The campsite is situated between a beautiful sandy beach and a nature reserve, in France's sunniest region.

◉ Beach on site
○ Beach within 1 km
◉ Sandy beach
○ Blue Flag quality
◉ Lifeguard *(high season)*
○ Sun lounger and/or deckchair hire
○ Watersports *(e.g. sailing or windsurfing)*
○ Snacks and drinks
○ Sunshades/sunbeds
◉ Dogs allowed *(on the beach)*

Facilities: Four fully equipped toilet blocks on le Floride and two on l'Embouchure where 50 pitches near the beach have individual facilities. Facilities for babies and disabled visitors. Family shower room. Motorcaravan services. Shop, bar, restaurant and takeaway (all 15/6-5/9). Excellent pool complex with indoor heated pool (all season). Excellent play area. Multisports court. Gym. Tennis. Sports programmes and multilingual entertainment (1/5-30/9). Bicycle hire. Charcoal barbecues are not permitted. Max. 1 dog. WiFi over site (charged). Off site: Beach 100 m. Fishing 1 km. Riding 1.5 km.

Open: 1 April - 30 September.

Directions: From A9 take exit 41 (Perpignan Nord) and follow signs for Canet and Le Barcarès via D83. At exit 9 follow D81 (Canet) then next left into Le Barcarès Village. Site is 1 km. on the left and right sides of the road.

GPS: 42.77855, 3.0301

Charges guide

Per unit incl. 2 persons and electricity	€ 15,00 - € 43,70
incl. individual sanitary facility	€ 19,00 - € 54,30
extra person	€ 2,90 - € 6,70
child (1-3 yrs)	no charge - € 3,90

France – Le Barcarès

Camping Club le Floride et l'Embouchure

Route de Saint Laurent, F-66423 Le Barcarès (Pyrénées-Orientales)
t: 04 68 86 11 75   e: campingfloride@orange.fr
alanrogers.com/FR66290   www.floride.fr

Accommodation: ☑ Pitch ☑ Mobile home/chalet ○ Hotel/B&B ○ Apartment

A well established and multi-lingual, family run enterprise, le Floride et l'Embouchure is really two sites in one – l'Embouchure the smaller one with direct access to the beach and le Floride on the opposite side of the road. Fifty pitches have their own individual sanitary facility and in total the site offers 632 reasonably sized pitches, 280 for touring, all with 10A electricity. A good range of chalets and mobile homes are available for rent, including a recent Polynesian-style village. It is relatively inexpensive, especially outside the July/August peak period and the majority of the comprehensive facilities are open from 1st May. The busy town of Le Barcarès is within easy walking distance and has an increasing range of shops and supermarkets. The Voie Verte tarmac pathway runs for 15 km. from Le Barcarès to Rivesaltes alongside the River Agly, which borders l'Embouchure and is popular with cyclists, walkers, runners and roller skaters.

You might like to know

The site has direct access to the sea (100 m) and to a 3,000 sq.m. aquatic complex with covered, heated swimming pool, paddling pool with games, a jacuzzi and fun slides.

- ☑ Beach on site
- ☑ Beach within 1 km
- ☑ Sandy beach
- ☑ Blue Flag quality
- ☑ Lifeguard *(high season)*
- ☑ Sun lounger and/or deckchair hire
- ☑ Watersports *(e.g. sailing or windsurfing)*
- ☑ Snacks and drinks
- ☑ Sunshades/sunbeds
- ○ Dogs allowed *(on the beach)*

France – Argelès-sur-Mer

Camping Club la Sirène

Route de Taxo á la Mer, F-66702 Argelès-sur-Mer (Pyrénées-Orientales)
t: 04 68 81 04 61   e: contact@camping-lasirene.fr
alanrogers.com/FR66560   www.camping-lasirene.fr

Accommodation: ☑ Pitch ☑ Mobile home/chalet ○ Hotel/B&B ○ Apartment

From the moment you step into the hotel-like reception area you realise that this large site offers the holidaymaker everything they could want, including a super pool complex, in a well managed and convenient location close to Argelès-sur-Mer and the beaches. There are 740 pitches over the 17-hectare site, and 520 mobile homes and chalets. They are modern in design, all less than five years old, and laid out in pretty avenues with flowering shrubs and shade from tall trees. There are now just ten touring pitches, with 16A electricity and water, and some 200 taken by tour operators. All the shops and amenities are near reception making the accommodation areas quite peaceful and relaxing. There is an amazing variety of activities on offer, and in the main season visitors have the option of using the free bus service to the beach where the site has its own club, Club Eméraude, where you can even go windsurfing at no charge, go kayaking, learn to sail a catamaran or just hire a pedalo. Back on the site, there is a diving club, scuba diving, snorkelling or a boat trip. There is daily entertainment for all the family.

You might like to know

An area of the North beach is reserved for dogs.

○ Beach on site
☑ Beach within 1 km
○ Sandy beach
☑ Blue Flag quality
☑ Lifeguard *(high season)*
☑ Sun lounger and/or deckchair hire
☑ Watersports *(e.g. sailing or windsurfing)*
☑ Snacks and drinks
☑ Sunshades/sunbeds
☑ Dogs allowed *(on the beach)*

Facilities: Two well equipped toilet blocks with facilities for babies and disabled visitors (key access). Laundry. Traditional restaurant and fast food bar, bar and takeaway, large shop and bazaar, large aqua park, paddling pools, slides, jacuzzi (all season). Games room. Two play areas. Multisports field. Four tennis courts. Archery. Minigolf. Football. Theatre, evening entertainment, discos, show time spectacular. Riding. Bicycle hire. Watersports. WiFi in bar area. Gas and electric barbecues only.
Off site: Resort of Argelès-sur-Mer with beaches, karting, 10-pin bowling, amusement park and the site's private Eméraude Beach Club, all 2 km. Interesting old town of Collioure close by. Fishing 4 km. Golf 7 km.

Open: 20 April - 28 September.

Directions: Leave A9 motorway at exit 42, take D114, towards Argelès. Leave D114, exit 10 and follow signs for Plage Nord. Site signed after first roundabout and is on right 2 km. after last roundabout.
GPS: 42.57093, 3.02906

Charges guide

Per unit incl. 1-3 persons and electricity	€ 26,00 - € 43,00
extra person	€ 6,00 - € 9,00
child (under 5 yrs)	€ 4,00 - € 6,00
dog	no charge

Facilities: Three toilet blocks (not open until July/Aug, except those beside pool). Motorcaravan services. Small supermarket (15/7-10/9). Bar, restaurant with takeaway (15/5-10/9). Outdoor swimming and paddling pools. Multisports court. Tennis. Minigolf. Boules. Playgrounds. Games room (1/5-14/9). Kids' club and programme of activities and entertainment (July/Aug). No electric barbecues. Communal barbecue. WiFi over site (charged). Max. 1 dog per unit. Off site: Riding and fishing 1 km. Bicycle hire 2 km. Beach with watersports (boating, sailing, windsurfing, water skiing, diving, jet skis) 1.5 km. Perpignan 18 km. Spain 50 km.

Open: All Year (excl. Christmas and New Year).

Directions: Le Barcarès is 50 km. south of Narbonne and 18 km. northwest of Perpignan. From A9 leave at exit 41 (Perpignan Nord) follow signs for Le Barcarès, after 10 km, take exit 9 towards Canet, Toreilles, then first right to Le Barcarès village. Pass under motorway and Les Tamaris is second campsite on left.

GPS: 42.77529, 3.020334

Charges guide

Per unit incl. 2 persons and electricity	€ 14,50 - € 34,00
extra person	€ 5,00 - € 7,00
child (4-6 yrs)	no charge - € 5,00
dog	€ 3,50

France – Port Barcarès

Camping les Tamaris

Route de Saint Laurent, F-66420 Port Barcarès (Pyrénées-Orientales)
t: 04 68 86 08 18 e: camping-tamaris@orange.fr
alanrogers.com/FR66890 www.camping-tamaris.com

Accommodation: ✔ Pitch ✔ Mobile home/chalet ○ Hotel/B&B ○ Apartment

Part of an extensive complex of campsites close to the pleasant village of Port Barcarès on the Mediterranean coast, and midway between Narbonne and the Spanish border, les Tamaris is largely dedicated to the 400 chalets and mobile homes (around 100 for hire), grouped in three concentric circles and in serried ranks. Just twenty touring pitches with electrical connections (10A Europlug) are available here but they are squeezed between the mobiles. The toilet blocks for the touring area do not open until July/August. The sandy beach is a 20 minute walk, as are the first of the shops, bars and restaurants of Le Barcarès. Regular markets are held here throughout the year and there is a busy port and marina. The Village des Pêcheurs pays tribute to the region's fishing heritage.

You might like to know

There is a choice of beaches within 7 km. with sun loungers, parasols, snacks and drinks. Don't miss Perpignan with its Castillet and Palais des Rois de Majorque.

○ Beach on site
✔ Beach within 1 km
✔ Sandy beach
○ Blue Flag quality
✔ Lifeguard *(high season)*
○ Sun lounger and/or deckchair hire
✔ Watersports *(e.g. sailing or windsurfing)*
✔ Snacks and drinks
○ Sunshades/sunbeds
○ Dogs allowed *(on the beach)*

Facilities: Ten modern, well used but clean toilet blocks. Mostly Turkish WCs. Facilities for disabled visitors (but steep steps). Baby room. Washing machines. Fridge hire. Well stocked supermarket, bars, pizzeria (all open all season). No swimming pool. Several excellent play areas for all ages. Activities and entertainment for children and teenagers (July/Aug). Tennis. Boats, pedaloes for hire. Wide range of watersports. New water games and fitness area. Multisports courts (one indoor for wet or hot weather) for football, basketball. Only gas and electric barbecues are allowed. Direct beach access. Dogs are not accepted 13/7-17/8. Free WiFi at the Tennis Bar (rest of site charged). Off site: Bicycle hire 2.5 km. Riding and golf 15 km.

Open: 28 March - 31 October.

Directions: From Bormes-les-Mimosas, head east on D559 to Le Lavandou. At roundabout, turn off D559 towards the sea on road signed Favière. After 2 km. turn left at site signs.

GPS: 43.11779, 6.35176

Charges guide

Per unit incl. 2 persons and electricity	€ 31,00 - € 49,00
extra person	€ 6,50 - € 11,50
child (2-7 yrs)	no charge - € 5,60
dog (not 13/7-17/8)	no charge

France – Bormes-les-Mimosas

Camp du Domaine

B.P. 207 La Favière, 2581 Route de Bénat, F-83230 Bormes-les-Mimosas (Var)
t: 04 94 71 03 12   e: mail@campdudomaine.com
alanrogers.com/FR83120   www.campdudomaine.com

Accommodation: ☑ Pitch ☑ Mobile home/chalet ○ Hotel/B&B ○ Apartment

Camp du Domaine, 3 km. south of Le Lavandou, is a large, attractive beachside site with 1,320 pitches set in 45 hectares of pinewood, yet surprisingly it does not give the impression of being so big. The pitches are large and most are reasonably level; 800 have 10A electricity. The most popular pitches are beside the beach, but those furthest away are generally larger and have more shade. Amongst the trees, many pitches are more suitable for tents. The price for each pitch is the same – whether smaller but near the beach, or larger under shade. The beach is the attraction and everyone tries to get close. American motorhomes are not accepted. Despite its size, the site does not feel too busy, except perhaps around the supermarket. This is mainly because many pitches are hidden in the trees, the access roads are quite wide and it all covers quite a wide area (some of the beach pitches are 600 m. from the entrance). Its popularity makes early reservation necessary over a long season (about mid June to mid September) since regular clients book from season to season. A good range of languages are spoken.

You might like to know

There is direct access to two different sandy beaches, one is very sheltered and ideal for children. Some of the pitches are directly on the beach; these are very popular so reservation is recommended.

- ☑ Beach on site
- ○ Beach within 1 km
- ☑ Sandy beach
- ○ Blue Flag quality
- ☑ Lifeguard *(high season)*
- ☑ Sun lounger and/or deckchair hire
- ☑ Watersports *(e.g. sailing or windsurfing)*
- ☑ Snacks and drinks
- ☑ Sunshades/sunbeds
- ○ Dogs allowed *(on the beach)*

Facilities: Two clean sanitary blocks with controllable pushbutton showers. Wet room for disabled visitors. Laundry facilities. Play area. Boules. New sports field. Mobile homes for rent. Dogs are not accepted 5/7-26/8.
Off site: Le Lavandou 500 m. Nearest beach 800 m. Bicycle hire 800 m. Fishing 1.5 km. Sailing 2 km. Golf 10 km.

Open: 1 May - 4 October.

Directions: From Hyères (A570) head east on D98 to Bormes-les-Mimosas and then southeast on D559 to Le Lavandou. Then follow signs to the site.
GPS: 43.136047, 6.354416

Charges guide

Per unit incl. 2 persons and electricity	€ 18,60 - € 30,50
extra person	€ 4,50 - € 6,60
child (under 7 yrs)	€ 3,20 - € 4,80
dog (excl. 5/7-26/8)	€ 2,80 - € 4,00

France – Le Lavandou

Camping Saint Pons

Avenue Maréchal Juin, F-83980 Le Lavandou (Var)
t: 04 94 71 03 93 e: info@campingsaintpons.com
alanrogers.com/FR83680 www.campingsaintpons.com

Accommodation: ☑ Pitch ☑ Mobile home/chalet ○ Hotel/B&B ○ Apartment

Camping Saint Pons enjoys an attractive setting within walking distance of the delightful family resort of Le Lavandou. This is a relatively small, quiet and uncomplicated site extending over two hectares, with many flowering shrubs and bushes. There are 155 pitches here, well shaded and of a fair size. All have electrical connections. A number of mobile homes are available for rent. There is no shop on site but there is a supermarket just 300 m. away. There is also a bar and restaurant next door. The Littoral cycle track runs close to the site and provides an appealing way of exploring the coast and a number of pretty Provençal villages. Saint Pons is a relaxed site with little by way of on-site entertainment which will be welcomed by many in this otherwise busy area. Le Lavandou is also one of the Riviera's more restrained resorts, named apparently after the river where local women came to do their washing because the water was so soft. The village boasts no fewer than 12 beaches, some wide and sandy, and others tiny, rocky coves. All can be reached by travelling on a small tourist train that runs along the coast.

You might like to know

There are no fewer than 12 beaches at Le Lavandou, including the Grande Plage, a fine sandy beach backed with palm trees.

○ Beach on site
☑ Beach within 1 km
☑ Sandy beach
☑ Blue Flag quality
☑ Lifeguard *(high season)*
☑ Sun lounger and/or deckchair hire
☑ Watersports *(e.g. sailing or windsurfing)*
☑ Snacks and drinks
☑ Sunshades/sunbeds
☑ Dogs allowed *(on the beach)*

MS Vacances Camping Club Le Trianon

95 rue du Maréchal Joffre, F-85340 Olonne-sur-Mer (Vendée)
t: 02 53 81 70 00   e: reservation@ms-vacances.com
alanrogers.com/FR85005   www.ms-vacances.com

Accommodation: ☑ Pitch ☑ Mobile home/chalet ○ Hotel/B&B ○ Apartment

Facilities: Three toilet blocks with controllable showers and washbasins in cubicles, facilities for babies and disabled visitors. Washing machines and dryers. Well stocked shop, bar and restaurant, snack bars and takeaway (all season). New water park with indoor and outdoor swimming pools. Fitness room. Massage and hairdressing. Adventure playground. Bouncy castle. Tennis. Basketball. Beach volleyball. Minigolf. Small fenced fishing lake. Bicycle hire. Activity programme (all season). Children's Clubs and entertainment at busy times. WiFi over site (charged). Only gas barbecues allowed. Accommodation for rent. Off site: Shops, restaurants and bars in Olonne-sur-Mer 1.5 km. Golf 2 km. Riding and Les Sables 5 km. Beaches (free shuttle bus in high season), boat launching, sailing and watersports.

Open: 11 April - 20 September.

Directions: Olonne-sur-Mer is 5 km. north of Les Sables d'Olonne. From A87 at La Roche-sur-Yon, head southwest on D160 towards Les Sables d'Olonne and leave at exit for Olonne-sur-Mer (D80). Continue on this road, crossing D760 and you will see the site (well signed) on right. Arrivals must use loop in car park opposite while booking in.

GPS: 46.53172, -1.758279

Charges guide

Per unit incl. 2 persons and electricity	€ 25,00 - € 47,00
incl. water and waste water	€ 30,00 - € 53,00
extra person	€ 6,20 - € 12,40
child	no charge - € 8,20

On the edge of the bustling village of Olonne-sur-Mer, close to popular resort of Les Sables d'Olonne, Le Trianon is a large site very much geared to mobile homes and chalets, of which 374 are available for rent. There are 68 touring pitches scattered amongst the statics. They vary in size and shape but all have water taps and drainage, with 10A electricity nearby; there is plenty of shade. The site is under new ownership and there are ambitious development plans. Nearby Olonne-sur-Mer has shops, bars, restaurants and a large supermarket. Free transport is provided to the beach in July and August. The new aqua park is highly impressive, with both indoor and outdoor pools, and no less than six waterslides, including the 'Space Hole'. The nearest beach is about 5 km. away, but there are many others to choose from, including Les Sables' famous Grande Plage. The amazing historical theme park of Puy du Fou and the delightful Venise Verte are both well worth the journey.

You might like to know

This peaceful, shady site offers plenty of opportunities for relaxing and for enjoying the many activities available. 10%* discount for reservations made before 31 December 2104. *Terms and conditions apply.

○ Beach on site
○ Beach within 1 km
☑ Sandy beach
○ Blue Flag quality
☑ Lifeguard *(high season)*
○ Sun lounger and/or deckchair hire
☑ Watersports *(e.g. sailing or windsurfing)*
☑ Snacks and drinks
☑ Sunshades/sunbeds
○ Dogs allowed *(on the beach)*

MS Vacances Camping Club Les Brunelles

Le Bouil, F-85560 Longeville-sur-Mer (Vendée)
t: 02 53 81 70 00 e: reservation@ms-vacances.com
alanrogers.com/FR85440 www.ms-vacances.com

Accommodation: ✓ Pitch ✓ Mobile home/chalet ○ Hotel/B&B ○ Apartment

Facilities: Six well maintained and modernised toilet blocks have British style toilets and washbasins/showers in cubicles. Facilities for disabled visitors. Laundry facilities. Shop, restaurant, takeaway and large modern, airy bar. Covered pool with jacuzzi. Outdoor heated pool with slides and paddling pools. Solarium. Tennis. Entertainment for all age groups. Bicycle hire. Max. 1 dog. WiFi over site (charged). Gas barbecues only. Off site: Riding 3 km. Good, supervised, sandy beach 800 m. St Vincent-sur-Jard 2 km. Golf 20 km.

Open: 11 April - 20 September.

Directions: Longeville-sur-Mer is 28 km. south from the A87 exit 32 at La Roche-sur-Yon via the D747 (La Tranche), D949 (Les Sables) and in 3 km, D91. Site is 3.5 km. southwest of the village and is signed from the D21 (Jard-sur-Mer).

GPS: 46.41330, -1.52313

Charges guide

Per unit incl. 2 persons and electricity	€ 25,00 - € 47,00
incl. water and waste water	€ 30,00 - € 53,00
extra person	€ 6,20 - € 12,40
child no charge - € 8,20	

This is a well managed site with a wide range of facilities and a varied programme of high season entertainment for all the family. A busy site in high season, there are lots of activities to keep younger children and teenagers happy and occupied. Les Brunelles has 607 pitches of which 121 are for touring units; all have 10A electricity and 40 also have water and drainage. Most are 100 sq.m. to allow easier access for larger units. The touring pitches are mainly level on sandy grass and separated by hedges, away from most of the mobile homes. A large aquapark provides a swimming pool of 1,000 sq.m. with indoor and outdoor pools, flumes, slides, a sauna, steam room, jacuzzi, and a fitness centre. Adults (over 16 yrs) can relax in the tranquil Zen pool. A good, supervised, sandy beach is 800 m. away.

You might like to know

There are three sandy beaches within easy reach, as well as surfing and sailing schools. 10%* discount for reservations made before 31 December 2104.
*Terms and conditions apply.

- ✓ Beach on site
- ✓ Beach within 1 km
- ✓ Sandy beach
- ✓ Blue Flag quality
- ✓ Lifeguard *(high season)*
- ○ Sun lounger and/or deckchair hire
- ✓ Watersports *(e.g. sailing or windsurfing)*
- ✓ Snacks and drinks
- ✓ Sunshades/sunbeds
- ○ Dogs allowed *(on the beach)*

Facilities: Three excellent toilet blocks include showers, WCs and washbasins. Kitchen with sinks, electric hobs and fridges. Laundry with washing machines. Small shop and restaurant. Sandy beach. Fishing, sailing and swimming. Communal barbecues. Free WiFi over part of site. Bungalows to rent. Dogs are not allowed on the beach. Off site: Riding, golf and bicycle hire 10 km. Sithonia, Mount Athos and the nearby Spalathronisia islands.

Open: 1 May - 31 October.

Directions: Although the postal address is Neos Marmaras the site is 12 km. south. Stay on main coast road, past casino resort at Porto Carras and 5 km. further on turn right towards the site (signed). Then turn right again down to coast and turn left and on for 1.5 km. Turn right into site access road. Reception is 700 m.

GPS: 40.024183, 23.81595

Charges guide

Per unit incl. 2 persons
and electricity € 34,20 - € 38,00

No credit cards.

Greece – Neos Marmaras

Camping Areti

GR-63081 Neos Marmaras (Central Macedonia)
t: 237 507 1430 e: info@areti-chalkidiki.gr
alanrogers.com/GR8145 www.areti-campingandbungalows.gr

Accommodation: ☑ Pitch ☑ Mobile home/chalet ○ Hotel/B&B ○ Apartment

If you imagine a typical Greek campsite as being set immediately behind a small sandy beach in a quiet cove with pitches amongst pine and olive trees that stretch a long way back to the small coast road, then you have found your ideal site. Camping Areti is beautifully located just off the beaten track on the peninsula of Sithonia. It has 130 pitches for touring units. The olive groves at the rear provide hidden parking spaces for caravans and boats, and small boats can be launched from the beach. The Charalambidi family maintain their site to very high standards and visitors will not be disappointed. Olive, pine and eucalyptus trees provide shade for the grassed pitches, and when we visited in mid June there was a wonderful display of cacti in full bloom by the entrance. The site, with its quiet, picturesque location, good facilities and friendly management has justly won many recommendations, and represents camping at its best; it is the ideal place to spend some time after the long journey down to Greece.

You might like to know

The Spalathronisia, three small islands ideal for excursions and fishing, are just 300 m. from the beach.

○ Beach on site
☑ Beach within 1 km
☑ Sandy beach
○ Blue Flag quality
○ Lifeguard *(high season)*
○ Sun lounger and/or deckchair hire
☑ Watersports *(e.g. sailing or windsurfing)*
☑ Snacks and drinks
○ Sunshades/sunbeds
○ Dogs allowed *(on the beach)*

Facilities: Excellent refurbished toilet blocks include showers, WCs and washbasins. Baby bath. Facilities for disabled visitors. Laundry with washing machines and ironing board. Electric hobs for cooking. Fridge and freezer. Small shop (1/6-30/9). Off site: Drepano beach, local tavernas and bars. Assini.

Open: 1 April - 30 October.

Directions: From Nafplio follow the main road west and then turn right towards Drepano. In the town follow the signs Plaka Drepano and turn left towards the coast. At the beach turn right and site is just ahead.

GPS: 37.53202, 22.89165

Charges guide

Per unit incl. 2 persons
and electricity € 24,00

Camping Triton II

Plaka Drepano, GR-21060 Nafplio (Peloponnese)
t: 27 52 09 21 28
alanrogers.com/GR8635 www.tritonii.gr

Accommodation: ☑ Pitch ☑ Mobile home/chalet ○ Hotel/B&B ○ Apartment

What do we look for in a good campsite in Greece? Given the excellent Greek weather, the answer is probably a good, flat pitch with some shade, excellent toilets and showers that are spotlessly clean, a small shop and proximity to a beach and local tavernas. Well, here you have it all! Under the control of the owners, Mr. and Mrs. George Christopoulous, this is an exceptional site with 40 good sized touring pitches under high screens, just across the road from Drepano beach. Local tavernas are within strolling distance and the town's shops are about a mile away. Personal management and supervision clearly works and this small site sets very high standards that others often fail to achieve.

You might like to know

Close to the Drepano beach are small pool areas where blue and white cranes live and breed. Deprano village is 1.2 km. away with a choice of tavernas and local bars.

○ Beach on site
☑ Beach within 1 km
☑ Sandy beach
○ Blue Flag quality
○ Lifeguard *(high season)*
○ Sun lounger and/or deckchair hire
☑ Watersports *(e.g. sailing or windsurfing)*
○ Snacks and drinks
☑ Sunshades/sunbeds
○ Dogs allowed *(on the beach)*

Facilities: The good toilet block includes showers, WCs and washbasins. Facilities for disabled visitors. Kitchen includes sinks, electric hobs and fridges. Laundry. Bar, small shop and restaurant. Accommodation to rent. Off site: Finikounda and the Inouse Islands. Distance to boat launching and sailing 3 km. Bicycle hire 25 km.

Open: All year.

Directions: Site is 3 km. from the centre of Finikounda. From the village head west and turn left into the site.

GPS: 36.802817, 21.78105

Charges guide

Per unit incl. 2 persons
and electricity € 21,00 - € 24,00

| extra person € 5,50 - € 6,00 |
| child (4-10 yrs) € 3,00 - € 3,50 |

No credit cards.

Greece – Finikounda

Camping Finikes

GR-24006 Finikounda (Peloponnese)
t: 272 302 8524 e: camping-finikes@otenet.gr
alanrogers.com/GR8695 www.finikescamping.gr

Accommodation: ☑ Pitch   ☑ Mobile home/chalet   ○ Hotel/B&B   ☑ Apartment

This site offers 80 level pitches with good shade and great views. It also has 16 apartments to rent. Some pitches have high reed screens that give good protection from the blazing Greek sun and the turquoise sea is great for swimming, windsurfing and sailing. The site is at the western corner of Finikounda Bay and has direct access to the sandy beach by crossing small natural dunes. The facilities are excellent and in low season, when there are 18 or less campers, each camper is given the keys to a WC and shower for their own personal use. The small picturesque village, three kilometres to the east, is at the back of the bay. Caiques and fishing boats are drawn up all along the sandy shore here, while tavernas serve their fresh catch along the water's edge.

You might like to know

An attractive path runs across the dunes from the site to the beach, which is excellent for children. The town of Finikounda is a 20 minute walk along the beach.

☑ Beach on site
○ Beach within 1 km
☑ Sandy beach
○ Blue Flag quality
○ Lifeguard *(high season)*
○ Sun lounger and/or deckchair hire
☑ Watersports *(e.g. sailing or windsurfing)*
○ Snacks and drinks
○ Sunshades/sunbeds
○ Dogs allowed *(on the beach)*

Facilities: The five toilet blocks are well situated and, even in high season, were kept very clean and never became overcrowded. Open washbasins, hot water to showers, and communal refrigerators and freezers. Small shop sells basic provisions (May-Oct). Other shops within walking distance. WiFi over part of site. Off site: Within walking distance of Gialova with its promenade restaurants. Pylos 6 km. Nestors Palace 12 km. Numerous places to visit. Golf 2 km. Bicycle hire 0.5 km.

Open: 1 April - 31 October.

Directions: Directly on the National Road Pylos Kyparissia. 300 metres from the village of Gialova.

GPS: 36.94764, 21.70618

Charges guide

Per unit incl. 2 persons and electricity € 22,00 - € 26,50	
extra person € 5,50 - € 6,50	
child € 2,50 - € 3,00	

Camping Navarino Beach

Gialova, GR-24001 Pylos (Peloponnese)
t: 272 302 2973 e: info@navarino-beach.gr
alanrogers.com/GR8705 www.navarino-beach.gr

Accommodation: ☑ Pitch ☑ Mobile home/chalet ○ Hotel/B&B ○ Apartment

There are 150 pitches, most facing the beach, with 30 being directly situated alongside. All have electricity (10A) and most have good shade. The pitches are arranged in rows to ensure that all have beach access. The facilities are adequate and cleaned regularly. The staff are friendly and efficient, and there is a very good restaurant with a terrace directly by the beach. The light wind in the morning, which strengthens on some afternoons, makes it a great windsurfing location and boats can be moored by the beach. This site is highly recommended. Situated directly on the beach in the historic Bay of Navarino, there can be very few sites in this guide that have the wonderful position this one occupies. It is superb and has the most amazing sunset to complement that. The site is split into two, with the section across the road used mainly for tents or as the overspill. There is plenty of shade. The beach is sandy and shelves gently making it incredibly safe for children.

You might like to know

The shallow blue water on this sandy beach is safe for children. The campsite recommend a visit to the Divary Lagoon, considered to be one of the most important lagoons in Greece.

☑ Beach on site

○ Beach within 1 km

☑ Sandy beach

○ Blue Flag quality

○ Lifeguard *(high season)*

○ Sun lounger and/or deckchair hire

☑ Watersports *(e.g. sailing or windsurfing)*

○ Snacks and drinks

☑ Sunshades/sunbeds

○ Dogs allowed *(on the beach)*

Facilities: The three excellent, well equipped sanitary blocks have child-size toilets and washbasins. Two bathrooms (hourly charge). Heated baby room. Facilities for disabled campers. Launderette. Dog shower. Motorcaravan services. Supermarket, souvenir shop and several bars (all 1/6-31/8). Restaurants. Children's pool (1/6-31/8). Massage. Hairdresser. Sports field. Minigolf. Fishing. Bicycle hire. Canoe, rowing boat and pedalo hire. Extensive entertainment programme for all ages. WiFi throughout (one free zone, elsewhere charged). Off site: Riding 3 km. Golf 20 km.

Open: 25 April - 28 September.

Directions: Follow road 71 from Veszprém southeast to Keszthely. Site is in Révfülöp.

GPS: 46.829469, 17.640164

Charges guide

Per unit incl. 2 persons and electricity	HUF 3750 - 7300
extra person	HUF 900 - 1250
child (2-14 yrs)	HUF 550 - 1000
dog	HUF 550 - 1000

Hungary – Révfülöp

Balatontourist Camping Napfény

Halász ut. 5, H-8253 Révfülöp (Veszprem County)
t: 87 563 031   e: napfeny@balatontourist.hu
alanrogers.com/HU5370   www.balatontourist.hu

Accommodation: ☑ Pitch   ☑ Mobile home/chalet   ○ Hotel/B&B   ○ Apartment

Camping Napfény, an exceptionally good site, is designed for families with children of all ages looking for an active holiday, and has a 200 m. frontage on Lake Balaton. The site's 370 pitches vary in size (60-110 sq.m) and almost all have shade – very welcome during the hot Hungarian summers – and 6-10A electricity. As with most of the sites on Lake Balaton, a train line runs just outside the site boundary. There are steps to get into the lake and canoes, boats and pedaloes for hire. An extensive entertainment programme is designed for all ages and there are several bars and restaurants of various styles. There are souvenir shops and a supermarket. In fact, you need not leave the site at all during your holiday, although there are several excursions on offer, including to Budapest or to one of the many Hungarian spas, a trip over Lake Balaton or a traditional wine tour.

You might like to know

There are grassy beaches at the lakeside, where pedaloes and boats are for hire. Fishing is also popular on the lake.

☑ Beach on site
○ Beach within 1 km
○ Sandy beach
○ Blue Flag quality
○ Lifeguard *(high season)*
○ Sun lounger and/or deckchair hire
☑ Watersports *(e.g. sailing or windsurfing)*
○ Snacks and drinks
○ Sunshades/sunbeds
○ Dogs allowed *(on the beach)*

Facilities: The toilet block (keys provided on deposit) is clean and fresh with hot showers (token €1.50), electric hand dryers and hairdryer. New reception building, including TV room, games room, campers' kitchen, laundry and a well equipped facility for disabled visitors. WiFi over part of site (charged). Automatic gate and door control. Off site: Children's playground adjacent. Public transport from village. Shops, restaurants, takeaway, pubs and ATM are just beyond the park's boundary in the village. Strandhill golf course 500 m. Bicycle hire within 1 km. Riding 2 km. Swimming pool and sports centre in Sligo 8 km.

Open: Easter - 30 September.

Directions: Strandhill is 8 km. west of Sligo city on the R292. Site is on the airport road.

GPS: 54.27242, -8.60448

Charges guide

Per unit incl. 2 persons € 20,00	
plus 2 children € 22,00	
electricity (10A) € 4,00	
extra person € 3,00 - € 5,00	

Ireland – Strandhill

Strandhill Caravan & Camping Park

Strandhill (Co. Sligo)
t: 071 916 8111 e: strandhillcvp@eircom.net
alanrogers.com/IR8695 www.sligocaravanandcamping.ie/strandhill_park.html

Accommodation: ☑ Pitch ○ Mobile home/chalet ○ Hotel/B&B ○ Apartment

This seaside park is located on 20 acres of undulating grass on a sandy base, with natural protection from the onshore breezes of the famous Strandhill beach. There are 55 hardstanding pitches for caravans and motorcaravans, with electricity and ample water points, and two camping areas for tents, one with views of the sea and the second more sheltered. Throughout the site many hollows provide ideal pitches for tents. Strandhill, world recognised as a surfing Mecca, also provides activities for all the family. There are miles of sandy beach and dunes, and the Knocknarea Mountain is a popular choice for walkers. The Megalithic Tombs at Carrowmore, older than the Pyramids at Giza, are 5 km. away and the flat beach at Culleenmore is 2 km. Strandhill provides an excellent touring base for the Benbulban, Yeats' Country and Lough Gill's Isle of Inisfree combining nature, heritage, and fable. There are two flights daily into nearby Sligo airport.

You might like to know

Swimming is not advised at this beach due to strong tides and currents.

- ☑ Beach on site
- ○ Beach within 1 km
- ☑ Sandy beach
- ○ Blue Flag quality
- ○ Lifeguard *(high season)*
- ○ Sun lounger and/or deckchair hire
- ☑ Watersports *(e.g. sailing or windsurfing)*
- ☑ Snacks and drinks
- ○ Sunshades/sunbeds
- ○ Dogs allowed *(on the beach)*

Facilities:
Facilities: Two modern toilet blocks serve the site, one at the entrance gate beside reception and the other in a central position. Heated facilities include WCs, washbasins and hot showers (on payment). Hairdryers. Laundry with irons and ironing boards. En-suite facilities for disabled visitors at reception block. Play area. TV/games room. Watersports enthusiasts can enjoy surfing, kite surfing, canoeing and board sailing on Keel Strand and Lough. Fishing trips can be arranged. WiFi throughout (charged). Off site: Bicycle hire and golf 200 m. Riding 6 km. In the village there is a food shop, takeaway, restaurants and music at night in the pubs.

Open: Easter - mid September.

Directions: From Achill Sound follow the R319 for 13 km. Site is on the left before Keel village.

GPS: 53.97535, -10.0779

Charges guide

Per unit incl. 2 persons and electricity € 18,00 - € 21,00	
child € 2,00	
extra person € 3,00	

Ireland – Keel

Keel Sandybanks Touring Park

Keel, Achill Island (Co. Mayo)
t: 098 432 11   e: info@achillcamping.com
alanrogers.com/IR8730   www.achillcamping.com

Accommodation: ☑ Pitch ☑ Mobile home/chalet ○ Hotel/B&B ○ Apartment

This is a park offering a taste of island life and the opportunity to relax in dramatic, scenic surroundings. Achill, Ireland's largest island, is 24 km. long and 19 km. wide and is connected to the mainland by a bridge. The wide open site is situated beside the Blue Flag beach near Keel village. Although there are static holiday mobile homes on this site, the 84 touring pitches are kept separate. There are 50 pitches with hardstanding and some are located at the perimeter fence overlooking the beach. Although sand based, the ground is firm and level. Roads are tarmac and there is direct access to the beach which is supervised by lifeguards. Occasionally a traditional music evening is organised on the site. Whilst a treat in store for visitors is the natural beauty of Achill, also worth seeing are Kildownet Castle, the Slievemore deserted village and the Seal Caves.

You might like to know

Achill is a haven for watersports enthusiasts, and keen golfers can play a round on the 9-hole course near the site.

- ☑ Beach on site
- ○ Beach within 1 km
- ☑ Sandy beach
- ☑ Blue Flag quality
- ○ Lifeguard *(high season)*
- ○ Sun lounger and/or deckchair hire
- ☑ Watersports *(e.g. sailing or windsurfing)*
- ○ Snacks and drinks
- ○ Sunshades/sunbeds
- ☑ Dogs allowed *(on the beach)*

Facilities: The toilet block is spotless. Laundry room. Campers' kitchen including toaster, microwave and TV. Shop (June-Aug). Fresh milk and bread daily. Mobile homes for rent. Sun/TV room. Free WiFi over site. Courtesy bicycles. Off site: Walking, beach and fishing. Boat slipway 2.5 km. Pitch and putt 2 km. Riding 6 km. Pubs and restaurants. The JFK Arboretum, Johnstown Castle and Gardens, the Irish National Heritage Park, Kilmore Quay and Marina, and Curracloe beach (featured in the film Saving Private Ryan).

Open: Mid March - 31 October.

Directions: From the N25 south of Wexford town, outside village of Tagoat, follow signs for Lady's Island and Carne. After 3 km. pass Butler's Bar and take next left and continue for 2.5 km. Site is well signed.

GPS: 52.206433, -6.356417

Charges guide

Per unit incl. 2 persons
and electricity € 20,00 - € 24,00

extra person € 2,50

child (2-16 yrs) € 1,50

Ireland – Rosslare

Saint Margaret's Beach Touring Park

Lady's Island, Rosslare Harbour (Co. Wexford)
t: 053 913 1169 e: info@campingstmargarets.ie
alanrogers.com/IR9170 www.campingstmargarets.ie

Accommodation: ☑ Pitch ☑ Mobile home/chalet ○ Hotel/B&B ○ Apartment

'This park is loved', was how a Swedish visitor described this family run, environmentally friendly caravan and camping park, the first the visitor meets near the Rosslare ferry port. Landscaping with flowering containers and maze-like sheltered camping areas and a pretty sanitary block all demonstrate the Traynor family's attention to detail. The 27 touring pitches all have 6/10A electricity, are sheltered from the fresh sea breeze and ferries can be seen crossing the Irish sea. Just metres away, the safe, sandy beach (part of the Wexford coastal path) curves around in a horseshoe shape ending in a small pier and slipway. Tourist information on the area is provided in the shop. The immediate area boasts of thatched roof cottages and cottage gardens. The park is an ideal base from which to explore the sunny southeast or as an overnight stop to prepare for touring Ireland or for departure. Local lakes and the Saltee Islands, various locations of ornithological interest, deep sea and shore fishing, and award-winning pubs and restaurants provide something for everyone.

You might like to know

The safe sandy beach is on the Wexford Coastal path. Lady's Island and lake, the site of an ancient monastry, can be found along the coast. Also recommended are Kilmore Quay and Marina and Curracloe beach.

○ Beach on site
☑ Beach within 1 km
☑ Sandy beach
○ Blue Flag quality
○ Lifeguard *(high season)*
○ Sun lounger and/or deckchair hire
☑ Watersports *(e.g. sailing or windsurfing)*
○ Snacks and drinks
○ Sunshades/sunbeds
○ Dogs allowed *(on the beach)*

Facilities: Three small and basic blocks provide toilets, washbasins and free hot showers. Laundry service for a small fee. Campers' kitchens and sheltered eating area. Restaurant and takeaway (July/Aug). Pets are not accepted. WiFi on part of site. Off site: Public transport from the gate during the summer months. Pub and shop 900 m. Riding 6 km. Golf 12 km. Boating, fishing and sea angling 200 m. Beach (pebble) 500 m.

Open: 1 April - 15 October.

Directions: From the N22, 17 km. east of Killarney, take the R569 south to Kenmare. In Kenmare take R571, Castletownbere road and site is 12 km.

GPS: 51.8279, -9.7356

Charges guide

Per unit incl. 2 persons and electricity	€ 21,50
extra person	€ 4,00
child (4-10 yrs)	€ 2,50

Ireland – Tuosist

Beara Camping The Peacock

Coornagillagh, Tuosist (Co. Kerry)
t: 064 668 4287 e: bearacamping@eircom.net
alanrogers.com/IR9580 www.bearacamping.com

Accommodation: ☑ Pitch ☑ Mobile home/chalet ○ Hotel/B&B ○ Apartment

Five minutes from Kenmare Bay, The Peacock is a unique location for campers who appreciate the natural world, where disturbance to nature is kept to a minimum. This five-acre site offers simple camping facilities. Located on the Ring of Beara, bordering the counties of Cork and Kerry, visitors will be treated with hospitality by a Dutch couple, Bert and Klaske van Bavel, almost more Irish than the Irish, who have made Ireland their home and run the site with their family. The variety of accommodation at Beara Camping includes a hostel, caravan holiday homes, secluded hardstanding pitches with electricity and level grass areas for tenting. In addition, there are cabins sleeping two or four people and hiker huts (van conversions) sleeping two, to avoid a damp night or to dry out. Bert and Klaske love to share with visitors the unspoiled natural terrain, its wildlife, the sheltered community campfire and advice on the walking and hiking routes in the area. The homely restaurant, open in July and August, boasts appetising and homemade food including breakfast with fresh bread each morning.

You might like to know

This site is situated on the beautiful Beara Peninsula, only 5 km. from Kenmare Bay. Here you will find marine and wildlife including seals.

○ Beach on site
☑ Beach within 1 km
○ Sandy beach
○ Blue Flag quality
○ Lifeguard *(high season)*
○ Sun lounger and/or deckchair hire
○ Watersports *(e.g. sailing or windsurfing)*
○ Snacks and drinks
○ Sunshades/sunbeds
○ Dogs allowed *(on the beach)*

Villaggio Turistico Europa

Via Monfalcone 12, I-34073 Grado (Friuli - Venézia Giúlia)
t: 043 180 877 e: info@villaggioeuropa.com
alanrogers.com/IT60050 www.villaggioeuropa.com

Accommodation: ☑ Pitch ☑ Mobile home/chalet ○ Hotel/B&B ○ Apartment

This large, flat, high quality site is beside the sea and has 500 pitches, with 400 for touring units. They are all neat, clean and marked, most with shade and 6/10A electricity, 300 are fully serviced. The terrain is undulating and sandy in the areas nearer the sea, where cars have to be left in parking places. A huge, impressive aquatic park covers 1,500 sq.m. with two long slides, a whirlpool and many other features, including a pool bar. This is a very pleasant site with a spacious feel which families will enjoy. There is direct access to the beach, where local tidal activity presents a large, protected area for children to play and paddle under the gaze of the lifeguards. The beach bar is pleasant and a narrow wooden jetty gives access to deeper water and the tour boats. This is a neat, well managed site setting high standards.

You might like to know

Various catamaran excursions to nearby nature reserves depart from the Villaggio Europa pier.

☑ Beach on site
○ Beach within 1 km
☑ Sandy beach
○ Blue Flag quality
○ Lifeguard *(high season)*
☑ Sun lounger and/or deckchair hire
☑ Watersports *(e.g. sailing or windsurfing)*
○ Snacks and drinks
☑ Sunshades/sunbeds
○ Dogs allowed *(on the beach)*

Facilities: Five excellent, refurbished toilet blocks are well designed and kept very clean. Free hot water in all facilities, mostly British style WCs with excellent facilities for disabled visitors. Baby showers and baths. Washing machines. Dishwashers. Freezer. Motorcaravan services. Large supermarket, small general shop (all season). 3 bars and 2 restaurants with takeaway (all season). Gelateria. Swimming pools (15/5-21/9). Tennis. Fishing. Bicycle hire. Playground. Full entertainment programme in season. Miniclub. Football. Basketball. Minigolf. Archery. Watersports. Dancing lessons. WiFi (charged). Dogs are restricted to specific areas and not allowed on the beach. Off site: Golf 500 m. Riding 10 km. Bus and boat excursions.

Open: 17 April - 21 September.

Directions: Site is 4 km. east of Grado on road to Monfalcone. Venice-Trieste motorway exit at Reipuglia-Monfalcone, first roundabout take second exit towards airport and follow Grado signs for 13 km. Site is on the left opposite a golf course.

GPS: 45.69649, 13.45595

Charges guide

Per unit incl. 2 persons and electricity	€ 19,90 - € 46,10
extra person	€ 5,70 - € 10,70
child (3-16 yrs)	€ 3,60 - € 9,70
dog	€ 3,20 - € 6,20

Less 10% for longer stays out of season.

Facilities: Five sanitary blocks, with all the usual facilities including free, controllable showers, washbasins in cabins, facilities for disabled visitors, children's area and baby room. Motorcaravan services. Bars, restaurants, pizzeria and ice-cream parlour. Supermarket and shopping centre plus first aid centre and a Murano glass shop. Swimming pools, paddling pools and hydromassage centre. Aquapark with waterslides (charged). Fitness centre. Solarium. Gym. Bowls. Tennis. Playground. Windsurfing school. Diving school. Games room. Entertainment and activity programme. Children's club. Excursions. Mobile homes and chalets for rent. Off site: Venice and Caorle.

Open: 21 April - 24 September.

Directions: From A4 motorway (Venice-Trieste) take exit to Ste Stino di Livenza and follow signs to Caorle joining the P59. Site is signed from Caorle on the continuation of this road to Porto Santa Margherita.

GPS: 45.56709, 12.7943

Charges guide

Per unit incl. 2 persons
and electricity € 13,00 - € 45,00

extra person € 3,00 - € 10,00

child (3-6 yrs) no charge - € 6,50

Italy – Caorle

Camping San Francesco

Porto Santa Margherita, I-30020 Caorle (Veneto)
t: 042 129 82   e: info@villaggiosanfrancesco.com
alanrogers.com/IT60110   www.villaggiosfrancesco.com

Accommodation: ☑ Pitch   ☑ Mobile home/chalet   ○ Hotel/B&B   ○ Apartment

Camping San Francesco is a large, beachside site in a quiet location close to the coastal town of Caorle (Little Venice), known for its connection with Ernest Hemingway. Although there are over 600 mobile homes to rent, 370 level, grassy pitches are reserved for tourers. They are close to the beach, shaded, and all have electricity (10A) and fresh and waste water connections. The site has every facility for a comfortable holiday, with swimming pools, an attractive aquapark (extra charge), a good beach for swimming, a large supermarket etc. However, some touring in the area from the site and a trip to Venice are also worthwhile. The large, well organised reception is supplemented by a separate information office at the flower-decked entrance to the site. At the end of the entrance road, near the fountain, are some shops and an ice cream parlour. The shop selling Murano glass will be of particular interest, especially if you are not already acquainted with the colourful products from the islands just north of Venice. The site has three restaurants, one at the beachside pool, and during summer there are entertainment programmes for children.

You might like to know

There are two beaches, only one of which is dog friendly. This has a designated water space and playground for dogs.

- ☑ Beach on site
- ○ Beach within 1 km
- ☑ Sandy beach
- ○ Blue Flag quality
- ○ Lifeguard *(high season)*
- ☑ Sun lounger and/or deckchair hire
- ☑ Watersports *(e.g. sailing or windsurfing)*
- ○ Snacks and drinks
- ☑ Sunshades/sunbeds
- ☑ Dogs allowed *(on the beach)*

Camping Union Lido Vacanze

Via Fausta 258, I-30013 Cavallino-Treporti (Veneto)
t: 041 257 5111 e: info@unionlido.com
alanrogers.com/IT60200 www.unionlido.com

Accommodation: ☑ Pitch ☑ Mobile home/chalet ☑ Hotel/B&B ☑ Apartment

Facilities: Fourteen superb, fully equipped toilet blocks; 11 have facilities for disabled visitors. Launderette. Motorcaravan services. Gas supplies. Comprehensive shopping areas set around a pleasant piazza (all open till late). Eight restaurants each with a different style plus 11 pleasant and lively bars (all services open all season). Impressive aqua parks (all season). Tennis. Riding. Minigolf. Skating. Bicycle hire. Archery. Two fitness tracks in 4 ha. natural park with play area and supervised play. Golf academy. Diving centre and school. Windsurf school in season. Exhibitions. Boat excursions. Recreational events. Hairdressers. Internet cafés. ATM. Dogs are accepted in designated areas. WiFi over site (charged). Off site: Boat launching 3.5 km. Aqualandia (special rates). Excursions.

Open: 23 April - 27 September.

Directions: From Venice-Trieste autostrada leave at exit for airport or Quarto d'Altino and follow signs first for Jesolo and then Punta Sabbioni, and site will be seen just after Cavallino on the left.
GPS: 45.467883, 12.530367

Charges guide

Per unit incl. 2 persons and electricity	€ 19,80 - € 51,70
with services	€ 22,20 - € 70,90
extra person	€ 4,90 - € 12,20
child (1-11 yrs acc. to age)	€ 2,90 - € 9,90

This amazing site is very large, offering absolutely everything a camper could wish for. It is extremely professionally run and we were impressed with the whole organisation. It lies along a 1.2 km. long, broad sandy beach which shelves very gradually and offers a huge number of sporting activities. The site itself is regularly laid out with parallel access roads under a covering of poplars, pine and other trees. There are 2,200 pitches for touring units, all with 6/10/16A electricity and 1,969 also have water and drainage. Because of the size of the site, there is an internal road train and amenities are repeated across the site (cycling is permitted on specific roads). You do not need to leave this site during your stay – everything is here, including a smart and sophisticated wellness centre. Overnight parking is provided outside the gate with electricity, toilets and showers for those arriving after 21.00. There are two aqua parks, one with fine sandy beaches and both have swimming pools, lagoon pools for children, a whirlpool and a 160 m. 'Wild River'. Another water park is planned for 2015.

You might like to know

One of Europe's largest sites, looking straight out to the Adriatic with a long (1,200-metre) private beach, Union Lido is a top quality holiday centre with a wide range of amenities.

☑ Beach on site
◯ Beach within 1 km
☑ Sandy beach
☑ Blue Flag quality
☑ Lifeguard *(high season)*
☑ Sun lounger and/or deckchair hire
☑ Watersports *(e.g. sailing or windsurfing)*
☑ Snacks and drinks
☑ Sunshades/sunbeds
◯ Dogs allowed *(on the beach)*

Facilities: Three toilet blocks are kept pristine and have hot water throughout. Facilities for disabled visitors. Washing machines. Large supermarket and shopping centre, bars, restaurants, cafés and pizzeria (all season; takeaway service 15/5-30/9). Excellent pool complex with slide and spa centre (all season). Tennis. Games room. Playground. Clubs for children. Entertainment programme. Direct beach access. Windsurf and pedalo hire. WiFi throughout (charged). Mobile homes, chalets and 14 eco-apartments for rent. Off site: ATM 500 m. Riding and boat launching 1 km. Golf and fishing 4 km. Walking and cycling trails. Excursions to Venice.

Open: 1 April - 30 September.

Directions: From A4 autostrada (approaching from Milan) take Mestre exit and follow signs initially for Venice airport and then Jesolo. From Jesolo, follow signs to Cavallino from where site is well signed.

GPS: 45.47380, 12.54903

Charges guide

Per unit incl. 2 persons and electricity	€ 20,00 - € 52,70
extra person	€ 5,00 - € 11,60
child (2-5 yrs)	€ 3,40 - € 10,20
dog	€ 2,70 - € 6,10

Italy – Cavallino-Treporti

Camping Village Europa

Via Fausta 332, I-30013 Cavallino-Treporti (Veneto)
t: 041 968 069 e: info@campingeuropa.com
alanrogers.com/IT60410 www.campingeuropa.com

Accommodation: ☑ Pitch ☑ Mobile home/chalet ○ Hotel/B&B ☑ Apartment

Europa is a smart, modern site in a great position with direct access to a fine, sandy, Blue Flag beach with lifeguards. There are 450 touring pitches, all with 8A electricity, water, drainage and satellite TV connections. The site is kept beautifully clean and neat and there is an impressive array of restaurants, bars, shops and leisure amenities. These are cleverly laid out along a central avenue and include a jeweller, a doctor's surgery, Internet services and much more. All manner of leisure facilities are arranged around the site. The touring area, with some great beachside pitches, is surprisingly peaceful for a site of this size. This site would be ideal for families. A professional team provides entertainment and regular themed summer events. Some restaurant tables have pleasant sea views. Venice is easily accessible by bus and then ferry from Punta Sabbioni.

You might like to know

There is direct access to a wide beach of fine sand, which is cleaned daily. It features natural dunes and is ideal for young children, while the new 'Roy Beach' welcomes dogs.

☑ Beach on site
○ Beach within 1 km
☑ Sandy beach
☑ Blue Flag quality
☑ Lifeguard *(high season)*
☑ Sun lounger and/or deckchair hire
☑ Watersports *(e.g. sailing or windsurfing)*
☑ Snacks and drinks
○ Sunshades/sunbeds
☑ Dogs allowed *(on the beach)*

Camping Marina di Venezia

Via Montello 6, I-30013 Punta Sabbioni (Veneto)
t: 041 530 2511 e: camping@marinadivenezia.it
alanrogers.com/IT60450 www.marinadivenezia.it

Accommodation: ☑ Pitch ☑ Mobile home/chalet ○ Hotel/B&B ○ Apartment

Facilities: Nine modern toilet blocks are maintained to a very high standard with hot showers and a high proportion of British style toilets. Pleasant facilities for disabled visitors. Laundry. Range of shops. Several bars, restaurants and takeaways. Five beach bars/snack bars. Enormous swimming pool complex with slides and flumes. Several play areas. Tennis. Surfboard and catamaran hire. Wide range of organised entertainment. WiFi (charged). Special area and facilities for dog owners (also beach area). Off site: Fishing 1 km. Riding 7 km. Golf 10 km.

Open: 12 April - 30 September.

Directions: From A4 motorway, take Jesolo exit. After Jesolo continue towards Punta Sabbioni. Site is clearly signed to the left towards the end of this road, close to the Venice ferries.
GPS: 45.43750, 12.43805

Charges guide

Per unit incl. 2 persons
and electricity € 21,10 - € 48,50

extra person € 4,70 - € 10,90

child or senior (2-5 and over 60)
€ 3,90 - € 8,70

dog € 1,50 - € 5,10

This is an amazingly large site (2,915 pitches) with every conceivable facility. It has a pleasant feel, with cheerful staff and no notion of being overcrowded, even when full. Marina di Venezia has the advantage of being within walking distance of the ferry to Venice. It will appeal in particular to those who enjoy an extensive range of entertainment and activities and a lively atmosphere. Individual pitches are spacious and out on sandy or grassy ground; most are separated by trees or hedges. All are equipped with 10A electricity and water. The site's excellent sandy beach is one of the widest along this stretch of coast and has five pleasant beach bars. The 15,000 sq.m. wide, multi-level AquaMarina Park has exceptional facilities - a feature pool for children with slides and a huge cascade complex, an Olympic size pool with massage jets, a lagoon with disability access, and a wave pool with a beach. There are charming features for the youngest campers, a choice of a whirlpool and a solarium on grass, plus an impressive 45-metre panoramic bridge. After all of this, enjoy a little relaxation on one of the reclining chairs and a refreshing drink from the bar.

You might like to know

The coast features natural sand dunes, golden sand and safe bathing. There are well trained and equipped lifeguards, and deck chairs and beach umbrellas for hire.

☑ Beach on site
○ Beach within 1 km
☑ Sandy beach
☑ Blue Flag quality
☑ Lifeguard *(high season)*
☑ Sun lounger and/or deckchair hire
☑ Watersports *(e.g. sailing or windsurfing)*
☑ Snacks and drinks
☑ Sunshades/sunbeds
☑ Dogs allowed *(on the beach)*

Facilities: Four modern sanitary blocks provide hot water for showers, washbasins and washing. Mostly British style toilets. Single locked unit for disabled visitors. Laundry facilities. Freezer. Motorcaravan services and stop-over pitches. Good shop. Bar/restaurant and takeaway. Outdoor swimming pool. Play area. Miniclub and entertainment (high season). Small zoo. Satellite TV and cartoon cinema. Watersports. Kayak hire. Fishing. Tennis. Bicycle hire. Communal barbecues. Torches useful. WiFi throughout (free). Off site: Boat launching 500 m. Bicycle track 1.5 km. Town with all the usual facilities and ATM 2 km. Riding 3 km. Golf 6 km.

Open: 5 April - 12 October.

Directions: From A22 Verona-Bolzano road take turn for Trento on S47 to Levico Terme where campsite is very well signed.

GPS: 46.00799, 11.28454

Charges guide

Per unit incl. 2 persons and electricity	€ 19,00 - € 52,00
extra person	€ 4,50 - € 9,90
child (3-11 yrs)	€ 4,00 - € 6,50
dog	€ 2,00 - € 5,00

Italy – Levico Terme

Camping Lago di Levico

Localitá Pleina, I-38056 Levico Terme (Trentino - Alto Adige)
t: 046 170 6491   e: info@campinglevico.com
alanrogers.com/IT62290   www.campinglevico.com

Accommodation: ☑ Pitch ☑ Mobile home/chalet ○ Hotel/B&B ○ Apartment

Camping Lago di Levico, by a pretty lake in the mountains, is the result of the merging of two popular sites. An impressive new reception has efficient systems and you are soon on one of 430 mostly grassy and shaded pitches. All pitches have 6A electricity, 150 also have water and drainage and 12 have private facilities. The lakeside pitches are really quite special. Staff are welcoming and fluent in English. The swimming pool complex is popular, as is the summer family entertainment. A small shop and a minimarket are on site and it is a short distance to the local village. The restaurant, bar, pizzeria and takeaway are open all season. A steady stream of improvements continues at this site which is great for families. The beautiful grass shores of the lake are ideal for sunbathing and the crystal clear water is ideal for enjoying (non-motorised) water activities. This is a site where the natural beauty of an Italian lake can be enjoyed without being overwhelmed by commercial tourism.

You might like to know

There is a large, private beach, but the clear, shallow waters of the lake offer opportunities for swimming, fishing, canoeing, and boating. Canoes and pedaloes can be hired from reception.

☑ Beach on site
○ Beach within 1 km
○ Sandy beach
☑ Blue Flag quality
☑ Lifeguard *(high season)*
○ Sun lounger and/or deckchair hire
○ Watersports *(e.g. sailing or windsurfing)*
☑ Snacks and drinks
☑ Sunshades/sunbeds
☑ Dogs allowed *(on the beach)*

Facilities: Two very clean and modern sanitary blocks near reception have British and Turkish style WCs and hot water throughout. Laundry. Motorcaravan services. Combined restaurant/bar/pizzeria/takeaway and shop. A swimming pool and paddling pool (1/4-31/10) and private beach. Tennis. Volleyball. Excellent play area. Wood-burning stove and barbecue. Fishing. Diving. Entertainment for children and adults in high season. Excursions. Bicycle hire. WiFi over site. Off site: Supermarket 200 m. Bus 200 m. Aquapark 500 m. Riding and golf 2 km. Ancient town of Albenga (2,000 years old) 3 km. Parachuting school 10 km. Local markets.

Open: 1 April - 20 October, 4 December - 10 January.

Directions: From the A10 between Imperia and Savona, take Albenga exit. Follow signs Ceriale/Savona and Aquapark Caravelle (which is 500 m. from site) and then site signs. Site is just south of Savona.

GPS: 44.08165, 8.21763

Charges guide

Per unit incl. up to 3 persons (over 2 yrs) and electricity	€ 23,00 - € 51,00
extra person	€ 6,50 - € 11,00
dog	€ 3,00 - € 5,00

Discounts for stays in excess of 7 days. Discount for readers 10% in low season.

Camping Baciccia

Via Torino 19, I-17023 Ceriale (Ligúria)
t: 018 299 0743   e: info@campingbaciccia.it
alanrogers.com/IT64030   www.campingbaciccia.it

Accommodation: ☑ Pitch   ☑ Mobile home/chalet   ○ Hotel/B&B   ○ Apartment

This friendly, family run site is a popular holiday destination. Baciccia was the nickname of the present owner's grandfather who grew fruit trees and tomatoes on the site. Tall eucalyptus trees shade the 106 flat touring pitches. Laura and Mauro work tirelessly to ensure that you enjoy your stay here and we have watched the growth of a very effective campsite over the years. An informal restaurant, overlooking the swimming pool and sports area, is cheerfully and efficiently run by Flavio and Pamela who serve delightful seasonal Italian dishes. The pool has a giant elephant slide which is always busy. There is a free shuttle to the site's private beach and the town has the usual seaside attractions. This site will suit campers looking for a family atmosphere with none of the brashness of large seaside sites. If you have forgotten anything by way of camping equipment just ask and the family will probably be able to lend it to you.

You might like to know

Baciccia is just 500 m. from the free beach, and 1.5 km. from the private beach (free shuttle bus).

○ Beach on site
☑ Beach within 1 km
☑ Sandy beach
☑ Blue Flag quality
☑ Lifeguard *(high season)*
☑ Sun lounger and/or deckchair hire
☑ Watersports *(e.g. sailing or windsurfing)*
☑ Snacks and drinks
☑ Sunshades/sunbeds
☑ Dogs allowed *(on the beach)*

Facilities: Seven new toilet blocks have hot water in washbasins (many cabins) and showers. Good access and facilities for disabled campers. Washing machines, spin dryers. Motorcaravan services. Gas supplies. Supermarket and general shop. Large bar. Restaurants, pizzeria and takeaway. Ice cream parlour. Swimming pool complex. Playground. Tennis. Windsurfing hire and school. Disco. Cinema. Gym. Excursions. Torches required in some areas. WiFi (charged). Dogs are not accepted. Off site: Bicycle hire 100 m. Fishing and riding 3 km.

Open: 18 April - 15 September.

Directions: The turn to Baia Domizia leads off the Formia-Naples road 23 km. from Formia. From Rome-Naples autostrada, take Cassino exit to Formia. Site is to the north of Baia Domizia and well signed. Site is off the coastal road that runs parallel to the SS7.

GPS: 41.207222, 13.791389

Charges guide

Per unit incl. 2 persons
and electricity € 25,50 - € 48,50

extra person € 6,50 - € 12,00

child (1-11 yrs) € 4,60 - € 9,50

Italy – Baia Domizia

Baia Domizia Villaggio Camping

Via Pietre Bianche, I-81030 Baia Domizia (Campania)
t: 082 393 0164 e: info@baiadomizia.it
alanrogers.com/IT68200 www.baiadomizia.it

Accommodation: ☑ Pitch ☑ Mobile home/chalet ○ Hotel/B&B ○ Apartment

This large, beautifully maintained seaside site is about 70 kilometres northwest of Naples, and is within a pine forest, cleverly left in its natural state. Although it does not feel like it, there are 750 touring pitches in clearings, either of grass and sand or on hardstanding, all with electricity, 80 now also with water and waste water. Finding a pitch may take time as there are so many good ones to choose from, but staff will help in season. Most pitches are well shaded, however there are some in the sun for cooler periods. The central complex is superb with well designed buildings providing for all needs (the site is some distance from the town). Restaurants, bars and a gelateria enjoy live entertainment and waterlily ponds surround the area. The entire site is attractive, with shrubs, flowers and huge green areas. Near the entrance is a new swimming pool complex with hydromassage points and a large sunbathing area. The supervised beach is of soft sand and a great attraction. A large grassy field overlooking the sea is ideal for picnics and sunbathing. Charges are undeniably high, but this site is well above average and most suitable for families with children.

You might like to know

The private fine sandy beach extends over 1,200 m. and offers a variety of services: pedal boats, canoes, windsurf boards, wake boards and water skiing.

- ☑ Beach on site
- ○ Beach within 1 km
- ☑ Sandy beach
- ○ Blue Flag quality
- ☑ Lifeguard *(high season)*
- ☑ Sun lounger and/or deckchair hire
- ☑ Watersports *(e.g. sailing or windsurfing)*
- ○ Snacks and drinks
- ☑ Sunshades/sunbeds
- ○ Dogs allowed *(on the beach)*

Facilities: Three sanitary blocks. One is newly renovated with private bathrooms, and facilities for children and disabled visitors. The two older blocks have mixed Turkish/British style toilets. Washing machine. Motorcaravan services (extra charge). Shop, restaurant and snack bar/takeaway (10/5-30/9). Live music concerts. Dog beach. Miniclub and entertainment in high season. Tennis. Water aerobics. Sailing. Sub-aqua diving. Windsurfing school. Riding. Torches essential. Bicycle hire. WiFi over site (charged). Communal barbecues. Off site: Riding 500 m.

Open: 20 April - 12 October.

Directions: Site is in southeast corner of Sardinia in the north of the Costa Rei. From coast road SS125 or the SP97 at km. 6, take the turn to Villaggio Capo Ferrato. Site is well signed from here.
GPS: 39.2923, 9.5987

Charges guide

Per unit incl. 2 persons and electricity	€ 22,50 - € 50,50
extra person	€ 5,00 - € 14,00
child (1-9 yrs acc. to age)	€ 2,00 - € 10,00
dog	€ 3,00 - € 6,00

Italy – Muravera

Tiliguerta Camping Village

S.P. 97 km. 6 - Loc. Capo Ferrato, I-09043 Muravera (Sardinia)
t: 070 991 437   e: info@tiliguerta.com
alanrogers.com/IT69750   www.tiliguerta.com

Accommodation: ☑ Pitch   ☑ Mobile home/chalet   ☑ Hotel/B&B   ○ Apartment

This family site situated at Capo Ferrato has changed its owners, name and direction (2011). The new owners have made many improvements, all of them in sympathy with the environment. The 186 reasonably sized pitches are on sand and have 3A electricity. Some have shade and views of the superb, fine beach and sea beyond. There are ten permanent pitches used by Italian units. The traditional site buildings are centrally located and contain a good quality restaurant using only fresh ingredients. This has a charming ambience with its high arched ceilings. Shaded terraces allow comfortable viewing of the ambitious entertainment programme. Cars must be parked away from pitches. The staff are cheerful and English is spoken. Consideration is given to the environment at every turn. There are numerous activities on offer – basketball, beach volleyball, riding and watersports, and in high season yoga, tai-chi, Pilates and dancing are possible. There is a full entertainment programme. We believe Tiliguerta is becoming a good quality, environmentally friendly site.

You might like to know

Tiliguerta is directly beside the sea, allowing guests to set foot on the sand without even leaving the campsite. It is the perfect place to enjoy one of Sardinia's most beautiful beaches, Costa Rei.

- ☑ Beach on site
- ○ Beach within 1 km
- ☑ Sandy beach
- ○ Blue Flag quality
- ☑ Lifeguard *(high season)*
- ☑ Sun lounger and/or deckchair hire
- ☑ Watersports *(e.g. sailing or windsurfing)*
- ☑ Snacks and drinks
- ☑ Sunshades/sunbeds
- ☑ Dogs allowed *(on the beach)*

Facilities: Two sanitary blocks include toilets, washbasins and free hot showers. No facilities for disabled visitors. Washing machine and dryer. Baby room. Motorcaravan services. Bar. Restaurant. Pizzeria. Well stocked shop. TV room. Bicycle hire. Tennis. Football and basketball pitch. New, comprehensive, well shaded children's play area. Entertainment (high season). WiFi (charged). Dogs are not accepted in July/Aug. Bungalows to rent. Off site: Sailing and boat launching 200 m. ATM in village. Riding 3 km. Golf 20 km. Costa Rei, Castiadas, Muravera, Villasimius.

Open: 1 April - 2 November.

Directions: Camping Capo Ferrato is in the southeast of Sardinia and can be reached by using the coast road towards Villasimius (SP17 or SS 125) then take the Costa Rei signs and the site is well signed on the southern edge of the village of Costa Rei. The site is in Costa Rei (Via delle Ginestre) and not on the promontory of Capo Ferrato.

GPS: 39.24297, 9.56941

Charges guide

Per unit incl. 2 persons and electricity	€ 22,20 - € 52,90
extra person	€ 5,60 - € 13,20
child (3-12 yrs)	€ 4,00 - € 9,90
dog (not July/Aug)	no charge

Special low season deals.

Italy – Muravera

Camping Capo Ferrato

Localitá Costa Rei, Via delle Ginestre, I-09040 Castiadas (Sardinia)
t: 070 991 012   e: info@campingcapoferrato.it
alanrogers.com/IT69770   www.campingcapoferrato.it

Accommodation: ☑ Pitch   ☑ Mobile home/chalet   ◯ Hotel/B&B   ◯ Apartment

Situated at the southern end of the magnificent Costa Rei, this small, friendly and well managed site has 83 touring pitches, many in great positions on the fine, white sand beachfront. They all have 3/6A electricity, are on sand, shady and of generous proportions. On the fringes of Costa Rei, the site benefits from close proximity to the shops and restaurants, yet enjoys absolute tranquillity. The charming restaurant holds it own against the village competition. This site is brilliant for beach lovers and windsurfers, and offers many watersports. It is reasonably priced and the beach shelves safely for children. The same family have been here since 1965 and the campsite was one of the first in Sardinia. In low season, special events are organised with other southern sites to enable you to 'feel the traditions' of Sardinia. Ask about the 'plein air' organisation. Close by is the Sette Fratelli Park with its mountains, canyons and woods, where you might be lucky enough to spot one of the many Sardinian deer.

You might like to know

The campsite overlooks the beautiful white sand and crystal clear waters of Costa Rei beach, which shelves gradually and is safe for children. Nearby 'Peppino's rock' marks a shallow bay ideal for snorkeling.

- ☑ Beach on site
- ☑ Beach within 1 km
- ☑ Sandy beach
- ◯ Blue Flag quality
- ☑ Lifeguard *(high season)*
- ☑ Sun lounger and/or deckchair hire
- ◯ Watersports *(e.g. sailing or windsurfing)*
- ☑ Snacks and drinks
- ☑ Sunshades/sunbeds
- ◯ Dogs allowed *(on the beach)*

Facilities: Two modern, heated, well maintained sanitary buildings provide roomy adjustable showers and some washbasins in cabins. Family shower room. Children's bathroom. Laundry facilities. Supermarket. Restaurant, bar and terrace. Separate takeaway. Swimming pool (unheated) and separate pool for children with slides and water features. Play areas and sports field. Boules. Volleyball. Children's entertainment (in holiday periods). Excursions for adults (low season). Bicycle hire. WiFi over site (charged). Off site: Beach 800 m. Fishing and riding 1 km. Golf 7 km.

Open: 1 April - 31 October.

Directions: From Westerscheldetunnel, turn right at roundabout to Breskens-Hoek-Oostburg. At Schoondijke roundabout follow Breskens/Groede, turn left at first lights to Groede/Nieuwvliet then right at first roundabout in Nieuwvliet. Site is signed. From Belgium: take N49 to Kaprijke and Breskens, entering NL at IJzendijke. At lights in Breskens turn left to Groede/Cadzand, and follow site signs.

GPS: 51.382207, 3.458188

Charges guide

Per unit incl. 2 persons and electricity	€ 20,00 - € 41,00
extra person (over 2 yrs)	€ 5,00
dog (max. 1)	€ 3,00

Netherlands – Nieuwvliet

Camping Zonneweelde

Baanstpoldersedijk 1, NL-4504 PS Nieuwvliet (Zeeland)
t: 0117 371 910   e: info@campingzonneweelde.nl
alanrogers.com/NL5530   www.campingzonneweelde.nl

Accommodation: ☑ Pitch   ☑ Mobile home/chalet   ○ Hotel/B&B   ○ Apartment

This family run site, only 600 m. from kilometres of wide, sandy beaches, is ideal for family holidays. Children will enjoy a walkway and a large slide through the dunes to reach the beach. There are 70 touring pitches, a wide choice of luxury holiday cottages and log cabins, plus places for 50 seasonal caravans. Electricity (10A) is available throughout. The Natural Reserve of Het Zwin is nearby (ideal for birdwatching) and many interesting villages are in the area. The landscape is perfect for exploring on bicycles along the safe, well signed routes. This site should appeal to children of all ages and features a character called Aartje Twinkel. Each year Aartje has a different theme (a popstar for example) which is the focus of the high season activities. The beach is within walking distance and carts can be hired to transport any equipment you take. There is an outdoor swimming complex which includes a pool and separate large area for younger children with slides and other water features. In low season there are excursions that have included day trips to Ghent and visits to cheese farms and other places of interest.

You might like to know

There is plenty of great entertainment for children here, particularly in high season, based at the Twinkelhuis.

○ Beach on site
☑ Beach within 1 km
☑ Sandy beach
☑ Blue Flag quality
☑ Lifeguard *(high season)*
☑ Sun lounger and/or deckchair hire
○ Watersports *(e.g. sailing or windsurfing)*
☑ Snacks and drinks
☑ Sunshades/sunbeds
☑ Dogs allowed *(on the beach)*

Facilities:
The three sanitary blocks are modern and clean, with washbasins in cabins, a baby room and provision for visitors with disabilities. Laundry. Motorcaravan services. Supermarket with fresh bread daily, bar, restaurant, takeaway (all 1/4-31/10). Recreation room. Swimming pool complex. Play area. Only gas barbecues are permitted. Dogs are not accepted.
Off site: Riding 150 m. Beach and fishing 300 m. Golf 6 km. Katwijk within walking distance.

Open: All year.

Directions: Leave A44 at exit 8 (Leiden-Katwijk) to join N206 to Katwijk. Take Katwijk Noord exit and follow signs to site.
GPS: 52.21103, 4.40978

Charges guide

Per unit incl. 2 persons
and electricity € 23,50 - € 31,50

extra person € 4,00

Netherlands – Katwijk

Recreatiecentrum De Noordduinen

Campingweg 1, NL-2221 EW Katwijk aan Zee (Zuid-Holland)
t: 0714 025 295 e: info@noordduinen.nl
alanrogers.com/NL5680 www.noordduinen.nl

Accommodation: ☑ Pitch ☑ Mobile home/chalet ○ Hotel/B&B ○ Apartment

This is a large, well managed site surrounded by dunes and sheltered partly by trees and shrubbery, which also separate the various camping areas. The 200 touring pitches are marked and numbered but not divided. All have electricity (10A) and 75 are fully serviced with electricity, water, drainage and TV connection. There are also seasonal pitches and mobile homes for rent. Entertainment is organised in high season for various age groups. A new complex with indoor and outdoor pools, restaurant, small theatre and recreation hall provides a good addition to the site's facilities. Seasonal pitches and mobile homes are placed mostly away from the touring areas and are unobtrusive. You are escorted to an allocated pitch and sited in a formal layout, with cars parked away from the pitches. However, with the super pitch your car can be parked on the pitch. Bicycles can be hired on site plus the nearby Space Expo is well worth a visit. The beaches are inviting and offer numerous possibilities for long walks and cycling tours.

You might like to know

The broad sandy beaches and sheltered dunes make this a beautiful area ideal for nature lovers, while being safe for young children.

○ Beach on site
☑ Beach within 1 km
☑ Sandy beach
○ Blue Flag quality
○ Lifeguard *(high season)*
○ Sun lounger and/or deckchair hire
○ Watersports *(e.g. sailing or windsurfing)*
○ Snacks and drinks
○ Sunshades/sunbeds
○ Dogs allowed *(on the beach)*

Facilities: One large and two smaller heated toilet blocks in traditional style provide separate toilets, showers and washing cabins. High standards of cleanliness. Dedicated unit for disabled campers and provision for babies. Warm water is free of charge. Dishwasher (free). Launderette. Motorcaravan services. Supermarket, snack bar, restaurant and takeaway (all season). Recreation room. Youth centre. Tennis. Playground and play field. Animal farm. Bicycle and children's pedal hire. Canoe, surf, pedal boat and boat hire. Fishing. WiFi over site (charged). Six cabins to rent. Off site: Golf 3 km. Riding 6 km. Beach 7 km.

Open: 28 March - 30 September.

Directions: From the Amsterdam direction take the A4 (Europoort), then the A15 (Europoort). Take exit for Brielle on N57 and, just before Brielle, site is signed.

GPS: 51.9097, 4.18536

Charges guide

Per unit incl. 2 persons
and electricity € 18,00 - € 25,00

extra person € 3,30

child (under 12 yrs) € 2,80

Netherlands – Brielle

Camping De Krabbeplaat

Oude Veerdam 4, NL-3231 NC Brielle (Zuid-Holland)
t: 0181 412 363 e: info@krabbeplaat.nl
alanrogers.com/NL6980 www.krabbeplaat.nl

Accommodation: ☑ Pitch ☑ Mobile home/chalet ○ Hotel/B&B ○ Apartment

Camping De Krabbeplaat is a family run site situated near the ferry port in a wooded, recreation area next to the Brielse Meer lake. There are 448 spacious pitches, with 68 for touring units, all with 10A electricity, cable connections and a water supply nearby. A nature conservation plan exists to ensure the site fits into its natural environment. The lake and its beaches provide the perfect spot for watersports and relaxation and the site has its own harbour where you can moor your own boat. This excellent site is very convenient for the Europort ferry terminal. Plenty of cultural opportunities can be found in the historic towns of the area. Because of the large range of amenities and the tranquil nature of the site, De Krabbeplaat is perfect for families and couples.

You might like to know

The campsite is in a beautiful, wooded area next to the Brielse Meer lake, just a stone's throw from the sea. It borders on a region of extensive polders, pretty villages and historical towns.

☑ Beach on site
○ Beach within 1 km
☑ Sandy beach
○ Blue Flag quality
○ Lifeguard *(high season)*
○ Sun lounger and/or deckchair hire
☑ Watersports *(e.g. sailing or windsurfing)*
○ Snacks and drinks
○ Sunshades/sunbeds
○ Dogs allowed *(on the beach)*

Facilities: Sanitary building with heating, washbasins in cubicles and baby bath. Facilities for disabled campers (key access). Washing machine. Microwave. Dishwasher. Motorcaravan services. Fresh bread. Animal corner. Sand pit. Boules. Books, magazines and toys to borrow. Activity programme during holiday period (3 times a week). Trampoline. Telephone. WiFi (free in games room). Dogs are not accepted. Off site: Restaurant opposite. Beach and fishing a few minutes walk over the sand dunes. Bus stop outside the entrance. Supermarket 50 m. Riding and bicycle hire 2 km.

Open: 28 March - 2 November.

Directions: Take the E312/A58 around the south of Middelburg then onto the N288 through Vlissingen and Zoutelande, after which the site is just over 1 km. on left.

GPS: 51.51046, 3.466318

Charges guide

Per unit incl. 2 persons
and electricity € 19,95 - € 31,70

Netherlands – Zoutelande

Camping Janse

Westkapelseweg 59, NL-4374 ND Zoutelande (Zeeland)
t: 0118 561 359   e: info@campingjanse.nl
alanrogers.com/NL7076   www.campingjanse.nl

Accommodation: ☑ Pitch ☑ Mobile home/chalet ◯ Hotel/B&B ◯ Apartment

Camping Janse is in the far southwest of Zeeland. It is a family, seaside site on the edge of sand dunes with the beach directly behind. There are 136 touring pitches, all 95 sq.m. with 6A electricity and water nearby, plus bungalows and caravans to rent. Some motorcaravan pitches are partly paved, and a field area (without electricity) is set aside for young people with small tents. Daily fresh bread is available and for other provisions the supermarket is 50 m. away. A restaurant with a terrace and play area for children is directly opposite the campsite entrance. In addition to the attraction of the sea and beach, there are opportunities for sports and activities on the site, and during the holiday period an organised activity programme runs three times a week. The site is on a cycle route and nearby there are walking and roller skating paths. Middelburg (13 km), the capital of Zeeland, has an historic centre and historic Veere (18 km) is a starting point for cruises on Lake Veere. The maritime city of Flushing is also well worth a visit.

You might like to know

This family site is just 2 km. away from the village of Zoutelande, and at the foot of the sand dunes.

☑ Beach on site
◯ Beach within 1 km
☑ Sandy beach
◯ Blue Flag quality
◯ Lifeguard *(high season)*
◯ Sun lounger and/or deckchair hire
◯ Watersports *(e.g. sailing or windsurfing)*
◯ Snacks and drinks
◯ Sunshades/sunbeds
◯ Dogs allowed *(on the beach)*

Facilities:
The clean, well maintained toilet block is modern with British style toilets, open style washbasins and hot showers, plus beach showers. Facilities for disabled visitors and babies. Laundry facilities. Motorcaravan services. Supermarket, bar with satellite TV (1/6-30/9). Restaurant and takeaway (1/6-15/9). Bicycle hire. Entertainment in high season. Charcoal barbecues are permitted. Off site: Beach and fishing 100 m. Bus service 800 m. Kayak excursions. Birdwatching.

Open: All year.

Directions: From the north, turn off the main coast road (N13-E50) just after camping sign at end of embankment alongside estuary, 1.5 km. south of ferry. From the south on N13 turn left at Hotel Faz de Minho at start of estuary and follow for 1 km. through woods to site.

GPS: 41.86635, -8.85844

Charges guide
Per unit incl. 2 persons

and electricity € 15,00 - € 31,30	
extra person € 3,40 - € 5,70	
child (5-10 yrs) € 1,70 - € 2,90	
dog € 1,00 - € 2,00	

Portugal – Caminha

Orbitur Camping Caminha

EN13 km. 90, Mata do Camarido, P-4910-180 Caminha (Viana do Costelo)
t: 258 921 295 e: infocaminha@orbitur.pt
alanrogers.com/PO8010 www.orbitur.pt

Accommodation: ☑ Pitch ☑ Mobile home/chalet ○ Hotel/B&B ○ Apartment

In northern Portugal, close to the Spanish border, this pleasant site is just 200 m. from the beach. It has an attractive and peaceful setting in woods alongside the river estuary that marks the border with Spain and on the edge of the little town of Caminha. Of the 262 pitches, just 25 are available for touring with electricity (5/15A Europlug), the remainder are occupied by permanent units and chalets for rent. The site is shaded by tall pines with other small trees planted to mark large sandy pitches. The main site road is surfaced but elsewhere take care not to get trapped in soft sand. Pitching and parking can be haphazard. Static units are grouped together on one side of the site. Water points, electrical supply and lighting are good. With a pleasant, open feel about the setting, fishing and swimming are possible in the estuary, and from the rather open, sandy beach.

You might like to know

The site is close to the Spanish border and just 200 m. from a beautiful sandy beach, ideal for swimming and fishing.

○ Beach on site
☑ Beach within 1 km
☑ Sandy beach
☑ Blue Flag quality
○ Lifeguard (high season)
○ Sun lounger and/or deckchair hire
☑ Watersports (e.g. sailing or windsurfing)
○ Snacks and drinks
☑ Sunshades/sunbeds
○ Dogs allowed (on the beach)

Facilities: Four clean toilet blocks (not all opened in low season) have mainly British style toilets, hot showers and mainly open-style washbasins (some with hot water). Washing machines and dryer. Motorcaravan services. Gas supplies. Simple shop (1/10-31/5). Supermarket, restaurant and bar with terrace (1/6-30/9). Excellent pool complex with paddling pool and large slide (1/6-30/9). Satellite TV. Games room. Playground. Tennis. WiFi in some areas (free). Off site: Bus service 100 m. Beach and fishing 700 m. Bicycle hire 9 km. Riding 10 km. Marinha Grande 10 km. Historic Leiria 20 km. Sailing and watersports 26 km.

Open: All year.

Directions: São Pedro de Moel is 140 km north of Lisbon. From A8 (auto-estrada do Oeste) at exit 24, take N242 to and through Marinha Grande; site is signed to the right on entering São Pedro de Moel.

GPS: 39.75806, -9.02588

Charges guide

Per unit incl 2 persons, electricity and water	€ 25,00 - € 39,00
extra person	€ 3,90 - € 6,50
child (5-10 yrs)	€ 2,00 - € 3,50
dog	€ 1,10 - € 2,20

Portugal – São Pedro de Moel

Orbitur Camping São Pedro de Moel

Rua Volta do Sete, P-2430 São Pedro de Moel (Leiria)
t: 244 599 168   e: infospedro@orbitur.pt
alanrogers.com/PO8100   www.orbitur.pt/camping-orbitur-s-pedro-de-moel

Accommodation: ☑ Pitch ☑ Mobile home/chalet ○ Hotel/B&B ○ Apartment

This very attractive and well kept site is situated under tall pines on the edge of the rather select small resort of São Pedro de Moel. It is a shady and peaceful place in low season, but can be crowded in July and August. There is space for some 400 touring units, including a few small marked pitches; otherwise you choose a place between the trees in one of two large camping areas; one has plentiful 6/10A electrical connections, the other very limited provision. A few pitches are used for permanent units and an area to one side has 120 chalets and mobile homes, mostly for hire. The attractive, sandy beach is a short walk downhill from the site (you can take the car, although parking may be difficult in the town) and is sheltered from the wind by low cliffs. However, this stretch of Atlantic coastline generally is wild (a surfer's paradise) and swimming should always be undertaken with care. The nearby town of Marinha Grande has all the usual services, including a good selection of shops, bars and restaurants, as well as a Museum of Glass. A little further away is the historic town of Leiria with trendy shops in the narrow streets of the old town.

You might like to know

The sheltered beach is only 600 m. away from the campsite.

○ Beach on site
☑ Beach within 1 km
☑ Sandy beach
○ Blue Flag quality
○ Lifeguard *(high season)*
○ Sun lounger and/or deckchair hire
☑ Watersports *(e.g. sailing or windsurfing)*
☑ Snacks and drinks
☑ Sunshades/sunbeds
○ Dogs allowed *(on the beach)*

Turiscampo

EN125, Espiche, P-8600-109 Lagos (Faro)
t: 282 789 265   e: info@turiscampo.com
alanrogers.com/PO8202   www.yellohvillage.co.uk/camping/turiscampo

Accommodation: ☑ Pitch ☑ Mobile home/chalet ○ Hotel/B&B ○ Apartment

Facilities: Two toilet blocks provide outstanding facilities. There is a third facility beneath the pool. Spacious controllable showers. Hot water throughout. Delightful children and baby room. Facilities for disabled visitors. Dog shower. Laundry facilities. Shop. Gas supplies. Modern restaurant/bar with buffet and mexican-style meals. Pizza bar and takeaway. Swimming pools (March-Sept) with extensive terrace and jacuzzi. Aquagym. Wellness facility. Bicycle hire. Entertainment on the bar terrace. Miniclub (5-12 yrs, 15/6-15/9). Two playgrounds. Boules. Archery. Multisports court. Cable TV. Internet and WiFi (partial coverage) on payment. Bungalows to rent. Off site: Bus to Lagos and other towns from gate. Praia da Luz village 1.5 km. Beach, watersports, sailing and fishing 2.5 km. Lagos 6 km. Riding 7 km.

Open: All year.

Directions: Site is 90 km west of Faro. From A22 Spain-Algarve motorway exit 1, follow N120 to Lagos then head west on N125, following signs for Luz. The impressive entrance is 3.8 km. on the right.
GPS: 37.10111, -8.73278

Charges guide

Per unit incl. 2 persons and electricity	€ 18,00 - € 35,00
extra person	€ 4,00 - € 7,00
child (3-10 yrs)	no charge - € 4,00
dog	€ 5,00

Turiscampo is an outstanding site which has been thoughtfully refurbished and updated since it was purchased by the friendly Coll family in 2003 and the transformation is on-going. The site provides 268 pitches for touring units, mainly in rows of terraces, all with 6/10A electricity and some with shade. There are 38 deluxe pitches with water and drain. The upper terraces are occupied by 132 bungalows for rent. Just down the road is the fashionable resort of Praia de Luz, with its beach, shops, bars and restaurants. Head west and the road takes you to Sagres and the wild western tip of the Algarve. Portugal's 'Land's End' has remained unspoiled and there are numerous rocky coves and little sandy beaches to explore. The headland at Cabo de São Vicente, has a working lighthouse and is well worth a visit, especially at sunset. Head east and you will come to the pleasant town of Lagos and beyond that, the whole of the Algarve with its beaches, little villages, fashionable resorts and bustling cities. This is a very good site for families, with wonderful facilities for children and plenty of activities in high season.

You might like to know

The campsite is 4 km. from Lagos and a little further is Portimão, both with superb sandy beaches.

○ Beach on site
○ Beach within 1 km
☑ Sandy beach
○ Blue Flag quality
○ Lifeguard *(high season)*
○ Sun lounger and/or deckchair hire
☑ Watersports *(e.g. sailing or windsurfing)*
☑ Snacks and drinks
○ Sunshades/sunbeds
○ Dogs allowed *(on the beach)*

Facilities: Five toilet blocks provide British and Turkish style toilets, washbasins with cold water, hot showers plus facilities for disabled visitors. Washing machines. Motorcaravan services. Gas supplies. Supermarket. Self-service restaurant and separate takeaway (June-Sept). Swimming pools (1/3-30/9). General room with bar and satellite TV. Tennis. Open-air disco (high season). WiFi over part of site (free). Off site: Bus from gate to village and to Faro. Beach 600 m. Fishing and bicycle hire (summer) 1 km. Golf 4 km. Spanish border 90 km.

Open: All year.

Directions: Quarteira is 19 km west of Faro. From A22 (Algarve-Spain) motorway take exit 12 for Quarteira and follow N396 to junction with N125 and turn east (Faro) then south for village of Almancil. In the village take road south to Quarteira. Site is on the left on stretch of dual carriageway - continue to roundabout and return.

GPS: 37.0673, -8.08712

Charges guide

Per unit incl 2 persons, electricity and water	€ 25,00 - € 39,00
extra person	€ 3,90 - € 6,50
child (5-10 yrs)	€ 2,00 - € 3,50
dog	€ 1,10 - € 2,20

Portugal – Quarteira

Orbitur Camping Quarteira

Estrada da Fonte Santa, avenida Sá Cameiro, P-8125-618 Quarteira (Faro)
t: 289 302 826   e: infoquarteira@orbitur.pt
alanrogers.com/PO8220   www.orbitur.pt/camping-orbitur-quarteira

Accommodation: ☑ Pitch   ☑ Mobile home/chalet   ○ Hotel/B&B   ○ Apartment

This is a large, busy, attractive site on undulating ground with some terracing, taking 795 units. On the outskirts of the popular Algarve resort of Quarteira, it is 600 m. from a sandy beach which stretches for a kilometre to the town centre. Many of the unmarked pitches have shade from tall trees. There are 659 electrical connections (10A on the older pitches, 16A on a group of new pitches at the far end of the site). Mobile homes are available to rent and there are others belonging to a tour operator. Like others along this coast, the site encourages long winter stays. A walk along the beach or a cycle (or bus trip) along the road takes you to the little resort of Quarteira where there are shops, bars and restaurants. A bus in the opposite direction will deliver you to the bustling resort of Faro where there are, of course, far greater opportunities for retail therapy and a wide choice of places to eat and things to do. The border with Spain is an easy drive along the motorway if you fancy a change of cuisine and a different shopping experience.

You might like to know

The city of Faro is a bus ride away – the bus leaves from outside the campsite gate; alternatively visit Almancil and the São Lourenço Church.

○ Beach on site
☑ Beach within 1 km
☑ Sandy beach
○ Blue Flag quality
○ Lifeguard *(high season)*
☑ Sun lounger and/or deckchair hire
☑ Watersports *(e.g. sailing or windsurfing)*
☑ Snacks and drinks
☑ Sunshades/sunbeds
○ Dogs allowed *(on the beach)*

Facilities: Three good sanitary blocks with facilities for babies and disabled visitors. Laundry. Cooking facilities. Motorcaravan services. Bar. Restaurant, pizzeria and snack bar with takeaway (21/6-4/8). Shop and kiosk (1/6-25/8). Minigolf. Play areas and adventure park for children. Boules and outdoor chess. Bicycle and go-kart hire. TV room. Beach. Fishing. WiFi over site (charged). Off site: Games, music and entertainment in high season. Tennis close by. Golf 1 km. Riding 3 km.

Open: All year
(full amenities 20 June - 5 August).

Directions: From E6 Malmö-Göteborg road take Torekov/Båstad exit and follow signs for 20 km. towards Torekov. Site is signed 1 km. before village on right.
GPS: 56.43097, 12.64055

Charges guide

Per unit incl. 4 persons
and electricity SEK 190 - 305

Sweden – Torekov

First Camp Båstad-Torekov

Flymossa Vagen 5, S-260 93 Torekov (Skåne Län)
t: 043 136 4525   e: torekov@firstcamp.se
alanrogers.com/SW2640   www.firstcamp.se

Accommodation: ☑ Pitch ☑ Mobile home/chalet ◯ Hotel/B&B ◯ Apartment

Part of the First Camp chain, this site is 500 m. from the fishing village of Torekov, 14 km. west of the home of the Swedish tennis WCT Open at Båstad, on the stretch of coastline between Malmö and Göteborg. Useful en route from the most southerly ports, it is a well situated site and worthy of a longer stay for relaxation. It has 535 large pitches (390 for touring units), all numbered and marked, mainly in attractive natural woodland, with some on more open ground close to the shore. Of these, 300 have electricity (10A) and cable TV, 77 also having water and drainage. The modern reception complex is also home to a good shop, a snack bar, restaurant, and pizzeria. The spacious site covers quite a large area and there is a cycle track along the shore to the bathing beach. Games for children are organised in high season.

You might like to know

At nearby Torekov, fishing boats are available to hire. Alternatively, take a short boat ride to Halland Vadero for a seal safari or to swim in the safe, shallow water.

☑ Beach on site
◯ Beach within 1 km
☑ Sandy beach
◯ Blue Flag quality
◯ Lifeguard *(high season)*
◯ Sun lounger and/or deckchair hire
☑ Watersports *(e.g. sailing or windsurfing)*
◯ Snacks and drinks
◯ Sunshades/sunbeds
◯ Dogs allowed *(on the beach)*

Facilities: Three heated sanitary blocks provide a good supply of roomy shower cubicles, washbasins, some washbasin/WC suites and WCs. Facilities for babies and disabled visitors. Well equipped laundry room. Good kitchen with cookers, microwaves and dishwasher (free), and sinks. Hot water is free. Gas supplies. Motorcaravan services. Shop (1/5-30/8). Pizzeria, licensed restaurant and café (all 1/5-30/8). Bar (1/7-31/7). Outdoor heated swimming pool (15/5-22/8). Playgrounds. Bouncy castle. Boules. Canoe hire. Bicycle hire. Minigolf. Family entertainment and activities. Football. Off site: Golf 500 m. Riding 2 km. Fishing 4 km.

Open: 12 April - 30 September.

Directions: Cross Öland road bridge from Kalmar on road no. 137. Take exit for Öland Djurpark/Saxnäs, then follow campsite signs. Site is just north of the end of the bridge.

GPS: 56.68727, 16.48182

Charges guide

Per unit incl. electricity SEK 175 - 430

Weekend and weekly rates available.

Sweden – Färjestaden

Krono Camping Saxnäs

S-386 95 Färjestaden (Kalmar Län)
t: 048 535 700 e: info@kcsaxnas.se
alanrogers.com/SW2680 www.kcsaxnas.se

Accommodation: ☑ Pitch ☑ Mobile home/chalet ○ Hotel/B&B ○ Apartment

Well placed for touring Sweden's Riviera and the fascinating and beautiful island of Öland, this family run site, part of the Krono group, has 420 marked and numbered touring pitches. Arranged in rows on open, well kept grassland dotted with a few trees, all have electricity (10/16A), 320 have TV connections and 112 also have water. An unmarked area without electricity can accommodate around 60 tents. The site has about 130 long stay units and cabins for rent. The sandy beach slopes very gently and is safe for children. Reception is efficient and friendly with good English spoken. In 2009 an outdoor heated pool and a children's pool were built at the entrance to the site. In high season children's games are organised and dances are held twice weekly, with other activities on other evenings. Nearby attractions include the 7 km. long Öland road bridge and the 400 old windmills on the island (in the 19th century there were 2,000). The southern tip of Öland, Ottenby, is a paradise for birdwatchers.

You might like to know

The gently sloping beach is safe for children and is cleaned daily. Youngsters will enjoy the Öland Animal and Amusement Park, just 3 km. away.

☑ Beach on site
○ Beach within 1 km
☑ Sandy beach
☑ Blue Flag quality
○ Lifeguard *(high season)*
○ Sun lounger and/or deckchair hire
○ Watersports *(e.g. sailing or windsurfing)*
○ Snacks and drinks
○ Sunshades/sunbeds
○ Dogs allowed *(on the beach)*

Facilities: Seven heated sanitary blocks provide a good supply of roomy shower cubicles, washbasins, some washbasin suites and WCs. Facilities for babies and disabled visitors (key at reception). Well equipped laundry rooms. Excellent kitchens with cookers, ovens, microwaves, dishwashers (free) and sinks. Motorcaravan services. Supermarket and bakery. Pizzeria, café, pub and restaurant. Takeaway. Bicycle hire, pedal cars and pedal boat hire. Minigolf. 9-hole golf course. Indoor/outdoor swimming pool (on the beach). Trim trails. Family entertainment and activities. WiFi. Off site: Fishing 4 km.

Open: 1 May - 1 September.

Directions: From Kalmar cross Öland road bridge on road no. 137. On Öland follow road no. 136 towards Borgholm and Byxelkrok. Turn left at roundabout north of Böda and follow campsite signs to Krono camping Böda Sand.

GPS: 57.27436, 17.04851

Charges guide

Per pitch SEK 155 - 285	
incl. electricity SEK 245 - 395	

Krono Camping Böda Sand

S-38773 Byxelkrok (Kalmar Län)
t: 048 522 200 e: info@bodasand.se
alanrogers.com/SW2690 www.bodasand.se

Accommodation: ✔ Pitch ✔ Mobile home/chalet ○ Hotel/B&B ✔ Apartment

Krono Camping Böda Sand is beautifully situated at the northern end of the island of Öland and is one of Sweden's largest and most modern campsites. Most of the 1,200 pitches have electricity (10/16A) and TV connections, 130 have water and waste water drainage. The pitches and 165 cabins for rent are spread out in a pine forest, very close to a fabulous 10 km. long, white sand beach. Here you will also find a restaurant, kiosks, toilets and beach showers, and a relaxation centre with an indoor/outdoor pool. The reception, the toilet blocks and the services at this site are excellent and comprehensive. Entertainment and activities both for children and adults are very extensive – there are more than 90 different items to choose from every week during high season. For exercise, there are tennis and badminton courts, trim trails, a football pitch and a nine-hole golf course (par 58) in the forest. Nearby attractions are the lighthouse at the northern tip of Öland, the Troll forest and the natural limestone sculptures at Byerum. Art galleries and craft shops are well worth a visit as well as the Swedish Royal family's summer residence, Soliden.

You might like to know

The white sand beach is cleaned daily.

- ✔ Beach on site
- ○ Beach within 1 km
- ✔ Sandy beach
- ○ Blue Flag quality
- ○ Lifeguard *(high season)*
- ○ Sun lounger and/or deckchair hire
- ✔ Watersports *(e.g. sailing or windsurfing)*
- ✔ Snacks and drinks
- ○ Sunshades/sunbeds
- ○ Dogs allowed *(on the beach)*

Facilities:
Three basic toilet blocks, 2 family rooms, facilities for babies and disabled campers. Launderette. Motorcaravan services. Supermarket. Gift shop. Café/bar/grill. Sports bar. Heated outdoor pool (20/5-1/9) and heated indoor fun pool with flume. Multisports court. Mini 10-pin bowling. Amusement arcade. Pool tables. Surf school (equipment hire). Two entertainment bars (one July/Aug). Kids' club for all ages. Soft play area. Playland. Road train. WiFi in bar area. Bus service. Off site: Golf and riding 1 mile. Fishing 3 miles. Newquay 8 miles. Eden Project 24 miles.

Open: 20 March - 31 October.

Directions: From Goonhaven take road for Perranporth. Site entrance on right before going down the hill.

GPS: 50.359357, -5.143635

Charges guide

Per unit incl. 2 persons and electricity £ 8.00 - £ 61.00	
extra person no charge - £ 2.00	
dog £ 3.00	

United Kingdom – Perranporth

Perran Sands Holiday Park

Perranporth TR6 0AQ (Cornwall)
t: 01872 573551   e: enquiries@haven.com
alanrogers.com/UK0135   www.haven.com/perransands

Accommodation: ☑ Pitch ☑ Mobile home/chalet ○ Hotel/B&B ○ Apartment

A large, bustling, commercial site set out amongst grassy sand dunes with over 1,100 pitches; 640 of these are for touring and there are numerous mobile homes dotted amongst the dunes. The dedicated touring area has its own wardens and a separate reception in high season. The park is a holiday village, with all the facilities that you could need – shops, restaurants, bars and entertainment. The entertainment centre is the heart of the site and is a long way from the camping areas. Pitches are on sandy grass, marked by fencing, some level, some sloping, many with rabbit holes. Most have 10A electricity and a few are hardstanding. A magnificent sandy beach is a stiff walk over some tall dunes. It is popular with surfers, but for something a little more relaxing there are indoor and outdoor heated pools on site, both with lifeguards. If you take advantage of everything on offer you won't need to leave the site, but the surfing paradise of Newquay is probably worth a visit, as is the Eden Project.

You might like to know

Perran Sands is a top surfing beach and the holiday park offers on-site surfing lessons and equipment hire.

○ Beach on site
☑ Beach within 1 km
☑ Sandy beach
○ Blue Flag quality
☑ Lifeguard *(high season)*
○ Sun lounger and/or deckchair hire
☑ Watersports *(e.g. sailing or windsurfing)*
☑ Snacks and drinks
○ Sunshades/sunbeds
☑ Dogs allowed *(on the beach)*

Facilities: Five modern toilet blocks provide showers, two family bathrooms, baby bath, laundry facilities and provision for disabled visitors. Well stocked supermarket with bread (from late May). Hire shop. Bars (with TV), restaurant, café and takeaway. Entertainment (every night in season). Pool complex with heated outdoor pool, paddling pool, sunbathing decks, solarium, sauna and massage chair. Health and beauty salon. Fun park, adventure playground, Kiddies Club. Amusement arcade and bowling alley. Teenagers' room. Par 3 golf course. 18-hole pitch and putt. Bicycle hire. Coarse fishing with three lakes. WiFi (free). Off site: Bus stop 200 yds. Riding within 2 miles. Bicycle hire and boat launching 4 miles.

Open: 10-24 April, 18 May - 13 September.

Directions: From A3075 approach to Newquay-Perranporth road, turn towards Cubert and Holywell Bay. Continue through Cubert to park on the right.
GPS: 50.384983, -5.128933

Charges guide

Per unit incl. 2 persons and electricity	£ 20.09 - £ 32.97
extra person	£ 6.27 - £ 11.96
child (3-14 yrs)	£ 1.73 - £ 8.68
dog	£ 4.60 - £ 5.90

Families and couples only.
Many special discounts.

Trevornick Holiday Park

Holywell Bay, Newquay TR8 5PW (Cornwall)
t: 01637 830531 e: bookings@trevornick.co.uk
alanrogers.com/UK0220 www.trevornick.co.uk

Accommodation: ☑ Pitch ○ Mobile home/chalet ○ Hotel/B&B ○ Apartment

Trevornick, once a working farm, is a busy and well run family touring park providing a very wide range of amenities, close to one of Cornwall's finest beaches. A modern reception with welcoming staff sets the tone for your holiday. The park is well managed with facilities and standards constantly monitored. It has grown to provide for caravanners and campers (no holiday caravans but 55 very well equipped Eurotents). There are 636 large grass pitches (600 with 16A electricity and 140 fully serviced) including TV connection, laid out on five level fields and two terraced areas. There are few trees but some good views. The recently refurbished farm buildings provide much entertainment, from bingo and quizzes to shows, discos and cabaret. Fishermen will enjoy the three lakes. The restaurant provides breakfast, lunch, dinner and takeaway food. There is an 18-hole golf course with a small, quiet club house offering bar meals; the views out to see are wonderful. Next door is the Holywell Bay Fun Park and the sandy beach is five minutes by car or a downhill walk from the park.

You might like to know

Surfing is one of the most popular sports in Cornwall and Trevornick Holiday Park is only a short walk away from the beautiful Holywell Bay beach, which attracts surfers from far and wide.

○ Beach on site
☑ Beach within 1 km
☑ Sandy beach
○ Blue Flag quality
○ Lifeguard *(high season)*
○ Sun lounger and/or deckchair hire
☑ Watersports *(e.g. sailing or windsurfing)*
○ Snacks and drinks
○ Sunshades/sunbeds
○ Dogs allowed *(on the beach)*

Facilities: Four basic toilet blocks with good hot water are spread amongst the terraces. The newer shower block has separate toilets. Shop. Self-service food bar providing good value meals and breakfast (main season and B.Hs). Two bars and full entertainment programme. Heated indoor and outdoor pools both with paddling pool areas. Fenced play area on bark with plenty of equipment. Ball area with nets. Crazy golf. Kingpin bowling. Off site: Riding next door. Golf, bicycle hire and freshwater fishing 0.5 miles. Beach 15 minutes walk or 0.5 miles.

Open: 24 March - 3 November.

Directions: Follow A361 from Barnstaple through Braunton towards Ilfracombe. At Mullacott Cross roundabout turn left for Woolacombe (B3343). Site clearly signed on left as you go down the hill into the village.
GPS: 51.17145, -4.191833

Charges guide

Per person (incl. electricity)	£ 10.00 - £ 20.00
child (4-15 yrs)	£ 3.50 - £ 10.00
dog	£ 2.75

Woolacombe Sands Holiday Park

Beach Road, Woolacombe EX34 7AF (Devon)
t: 01271 870569 e: lifesabeach@woolacombe-sands.co.uk
alanrogers.com/UK0735 www.woolacombe-sands.co.uk

Accommodation: ☑ Pitch ☑ Mobile home/chalet ○ Hotel/B&B ○ Apartment

This family park has sea views and is within walking distance of Woolacombe's lovely sandy beach. It is laid out in terraces overlooking the village and apart from its smart entrance, the grounds have been left natural. The pond and stream at the bottom are almost hidden with gated access to the National Trust fields across the valley. There are 200 terraced level grass pitches, all with 16A electricity. They are accessed by gravel roads with some good up-and-down walking needed to reach the toilet blocks and this may pose a problem for disabled campers. Some 50 mobile homes and 14 bungalows are in the more central area and tents tend to be placed on the bottom terraces. The park boasts both indoor and outdoor pools (accessed by code) with a full time attendant. Above the indoor pool is a very pleasant seating area with great views, with an outside seating area adjacent to it. Evenings see Woolly Bear emerge from his shack to entertain children, with adult family entertainment later. A good plus factor is the fact that all facilities open when the site opens.

You might like to know

Situated on the North Devon coast two miles west of Bideford, the BIG Sheep (a key member of Devon's Top Attractions) is an all-weather family attraction devoted to sheep and offering a wide range of indoor and outdoor activities.

○ Beach on site
☑ Beach within 1 km
☑ Sandy beach
☑ Blue Flag quality
☑ Lifeguard *(high season)*
○ Sun lounger and/or deckchair hire
☑ Watersports *(e.g. sailing or windsurfing)*
☑ Snacks and drinks
○ Sunshades/sunbeds
☑ Dogs allowed *(on the beach)*

Facilities: Three fully equipped toilet blocks – good provision for a busy beach park. Facilities for disabled visitors (Radar key). Baby care room (key system). Launderette. Bars with wide variety of entertainment and evening shows. Café. Good value supermarket and takeaway. Leisure complex with indoor pool, water play area for young children, gym and 10-pin bowling (family tickets available). Heated, supervised outdoor swimming and paddling pools (24/5-1/9). Activities for children. Two play areas. WiFi (charged). Off site: Bus stop on main road. Golf course 0.5 miles. Fishing possible from Chesil Bank. Abbotsbury Subtropical Gardens and Swannery 8 miles.

Open: 15 March - 9 November.

Directions: Park is immediately west of the village of Burton Bradstock, on the Weymouth-Bridport coast road (B3157).

GPS: 50.70500, -2.73867

Charges guide

Per unit incl. up to 6 persons, car and awning	£ 16.00 - £ 42.00
car or boat	£ 2.00
electricity	£ 2.00
small tent incl. 2 persons walking or cycling	£ 5.00 - £ 17.00
dog (max. 3)	£ 2.50

Single sex groups not admitted.

United Kingdom – Bridport

Freshwater Beach Holiday Park

Burton Bradstock, Bridport DT6 4PT (Dorset)
t: 01308 897317   e: office@freshwaterbeach.co.uk
alanrogers.com/UK1780   www.freshwaterbeach.co.uk

Accommodation: ☑ Pitch ☑ Mobile home/chalet ○ Hotel/B&B ○ Apartment

Family run parks for families with direct access to their own private beach are rare in Britain and this one has the added advantage of being in beautiful coastal countryside in West Dorset. It now offers the Jurassic Fun Centre with pools, gym, bowling and a café. This building has a living, 'green' roof supporting native species of salt-tolerant grass and wildflowers which helps the complex merge into the landscape, and includes many eco-friendly features. Approached by a fairly steep access road, the park itself is on level, open ground. The 500 touring pitches, 400 with 10A electricity, are on an open, undulating grass field connected by tarmac or hardcore roads. Caravan pitches are marked and evenly spaced in lines. Some tent pitches are in the main field, with others well spaced on a terraced field. There are 260 caravan holiday homes, with 60 for hire in a separate area. This lively holiday park has an extensive range of facilities, including an outdoor pool, a licensed restaurant and main bar with evening entertainment in season. Footpaths lead to the thatched village of Burton Bradstock and West Bay and the coastal path.

You might like to know

Freshwater has a private beach and is surrounded by coastal and country footpaths. There are indoor pools, 10-pin bowling, gym and seasonal entertainment, plus a shop, bars and a restaurant.

☑ Beach on site
☑ Beach within 1 km
○ Sandy beach
○ Blue Flag quality
○ Lifeguard *(high season)*
○ Sun lounger and/or deckchair hire
○ Watersports *(e.g. sailing or windsurfing)*
☑ Snacks and drinks
○ Sunshades/sunbeds
☑ Dogs allowed *(on the beach)*

Woodhill Park

Cromer Road, East Runton, Cromer NR27 9PX (Norfolk)
t: 01263 512242 e: info@woodhill-park.com
alanrogers.com/UK3500 www.woodhill-park.com

Accommodation: ☑ Pitch ☑ Mobile home/chalet ○ Hotel/B&B ○ Apartment

Facilities: Two modern toilet blocks with all necessary facilities including two family rooms with bath, showers, basin and WC, and four rooms with shower, basin and WC. Washing machine and dryer. Well stocked shop (19/3-31/10). Good, large adventure playground and plenty of space for ball games. Crazy golf. Giant chess and golf course adjacent to the site. Bicycle hire. WiFi throughout (charged). Off site: Beach 0.5 miles. Fishing and shop 1 mile. Golf and riding 2 miles. Bird Reserve at Cley. National Trust properties. North Norfolk Tourist Railway. Boat trips.

Open: 19 March - 31 October.

Directions: Site is beside the A149 coast road between East and West Runton.

GPS: 52.93742, 1.26250

Charges guide

Per unit incl. 2 persons and electricity	£ 16.10 - £ 20.15
extra person	£ 2.60 - £ 2.85
child (4-16 yrs)	£ 1.05 - £ 1.20
dog	£ 2.15 - £ 3.80

Woodhill is a seaside site with good views and a traditional atmosphere. It is situated on a clifftop, in a large, gently sloping, open grassy field, with 300 marked touring pitches. Of these, 210 have 16A electricity, seven are fully serviced and many have wonderful views over the surrounding coastline and countryside. A small number of holiday homes are available with magnificent sea views. Although the site is fenced, there is access to the clifftop path which takes you to the beach. Locally, it is possible to take a boat trip to see the seals off Blakeney Point. Nearby attractions include the Shire Horse Centre at West Runton and the North Norfolk Steam Railway. Green technology plays a major role with solar panels added to one of the block roofs to heat the water. Access to nearby towns and resorts is available using the local bus stop outside the entrance, or by the tourist railway.

You might like to know

The site overlooks a long sandy beach with rock pools - ideal for crabbing. There are several coastal walks to enjoy and nearby trips to see the seals at Blakeney Point.

- ○ Beach on site
- ☑ Beach within 1 km
- ☑ Sandy beach
- ☑ Blue Flag quality
- ☑ Lifeguard (high season)
- ○ Sun lounger and/or deckchair hire
- ☑ Watersports (e.g. sailing or windsurfing)
- ☑ Snacks and drinks
- ○ Sunshades/sunbeds
- ☑ Dogs allowed (on the beach)

Skipsea Sands Holiday Park

Mill Lane, Skipsea YO25 8TZ (East Yorkshire)
t: 0871 664 9812 e: skipsea.sands@park-resorts.com
alanrogers.com/UK4496 www.park-resorts.com

Accommodation: ☑ Pitch ☑ Mobile home/chalet ○ Hotel/B&B ○ Apartment

This well established holiday park is now owned by Park Resorts and is primarily dedicated to caravan holiday homes, of which there are 625 privately owned and 70 to rent. There is however a pleasantly laid out touring park occupying its own corner of the site and bordered by an attractive duck pond and a large playing area (both well fenced). The 91 marked, level pitches (some occupied by seasonal caravans) are separated by hedges and all have 16A electricity; some also have water, drainage and sewerage connections. The leisure facilities are outstanding and a full daily programme of activities and entertainment is offered for children and adults. Situated on the cliffs on the Yorkshire coast, south of Bridlington, beaches are either a good walk or a short drive away. There is a wide choice of possible days out: Beverley or York, each with its Minster and its horse racing; Spurn Point or Bempton Cliffs (RSPB); Cruckley Animal Farm or Bondville Miniature Village; Bridlington's beaches and its Harbour Heritage Museum; even Pickering and the North York Moors are within easy reach.

You might like to know

There is a good choice of beaches within easy reach of the campsite, including the popular family resorts of Bridlington and Scarborough.

○ Beach on site
☑ Beach within 1 km
☑ Sandy beach
○ Blue Flag quality
○ Lifeguard *(high season)*
○ Sun lounger and/or deckchair hire
○ Watersports *(e.g. sailing or windsurfing)*
○ Snacks and drinks
○ Sunshades/sunbeds
☑ Dogs allowed *(on the beach)*

Facilities: Two heated toilet blocks have been refurbished, with pushbutton showers, open washbasins and en-suite facilities for disabled visitors. Basic chemical disposal and motorcaravan service point. Washing machines and dryers. Well stocked shop. Bar, coffee shop and restaurant with takeaway. Leisure centre with sports hall, 10-pin bowling, heated indoor swimming pool, jacuzzi, sauna and steam room. Fitness centre with gym and snubbed. Games Kingdom with electronic games and Kids' Zone. Fishing in duck pond (charged). WiFi (charged). Off site: Buses from park gates. Village with shops, pub, restaurant 1 mile. Beach 0.25 mile (on foot) or 4 miles (by car). Golf 3 miles. Boat launching 6 miles. Riding and sailing 9 miles.

Open: 1 March - 31 October.

Directions: Skipsea is 20 miles northeast of Hull and 10 miles south of Bridlington. From Humber Bridge or from M62, take A63 to Hull, east of city follow signs to join A165 towards Bridlington. After 18 miles, turn east on B1249 to Skipsea. In village, turn right then left to site.

GPS: 53.98957, -0.20716

Charges guide

Per unit incl. all services	£ 11.00 - £ 46.00
tent pitch	£ 7.00 - £ 39.00
dog	£ 1.00 - £ 3.00

Facilities: The toilet block is of an excellent standard including washbasins in cubicles, facilities for disabled visitors and a baby room. Fully equipped laundry room. Dishwashing room and further sinks under cover. Motorcaravan services. Gas available. Local tradesmen visit each morning selling milk, bread and newspapers. New play area. Riding. Dry ski slope. Toboggan ride. Late arrivals area (with electricity). Off site: Amenities of the country park. Shops 1 and 2.5 miles. Beach 1 mile (dogs are restricted on the beach May-Sept). Jack Nicklaus-designed golf course 4 miles.

Open: 23 March - 7 January.

Directions: Leave M4 at exit 48 onto A4138 (Llanelli). After 4 miles turn right onto A484 at roundabout (Carmarthen). Continue for 7 miles to Pembrey. Follow brown country park signs in preference to sat nav. The country park is signed off the A484 in Pembrey village; site entrance is on right 100 yds. before park gates.

GPS: 51.6823, -4.2979

Charges guide

Per person	£ 5.90 - £ 8.00
child (5-17 yrs)	£ 1.60 - £ 3.10
pitch incl. electricity (non-member)	£ 16.20 - £ 19.90

United Kingdom – Llanelli

Pembrey Country Park Caravan Club Site

Pembrey, Llanelli SA16 0EJ (Carmarthenshire)
t: 01554 834369
alanrogers.com/UK5940   www.caravanclub.co.uk

Accommodation: ☑ Pitch   ☑ Mobile home/chalet   ○ Hotel/B&B   ○ Apartment

Set on the edge of a 520-acre country park, this popular Caravan Club site enjoys a wonderful location with a vast range of outdoor activities, including the use of a seven-mile stretch of safe, sandy beach a mile away. Well sheltered, the site is set in 12-acre grounds and provides 130 touring pitches, of which 68 are on hardstanding. All are equipped with 16A electricity. Thoughtful landscaping has included the planting of many species of trees. Sensibly placed service points provide fresh water and waste disposal of all types. RAF jets do practise in this area (although becoming less frequent and generally not at the weekend). There may be occasional noise from the nearby motor racing circuit. However, the real plus for this site is its proximity to the Country Park – access to this is free on foot or bicycle direct from the site, or reception can organise a weekly car pass for around £12. Within the parkland are walks, cycle trails, bird hides, an equestrian centre, adventure play area, dry ski slope and toboggan run, crazy golf and pitch and putt, miniature railway, bicycle hire and picnic areas, all fronted by Cefn Sidan, a seven-mile stretch of golden sands.

You might like to know

Cefn Sidan beach, an 8-mile stretch of golden sand described as one of Europe's best beaches, is approximately one mile from the campsite.

○ Beach on site
○ Beach within 1 km
☑ Sandy beach
☑ Blue Flag quality
☑ Lifeguard *(high season)*
○ Sun lounger and/or deckchair hire
○ Watersports *(e.g. sailing or windsurfing)*
○ Snacks and drinks
○ Sunshades/sunbeds
○ Dogs allowed *(on the beach)*

Facilities: The single prefabricated toilet block is clean, heated and adequate. No specific facilities for disabled visitors or babies. Laundry facilities. Games room. Direct beach access. Sea swimming and fishing. Canoeing. WiFi (in the games room; charged). Accommodation to rent. Off site: Well stocked village shop 100 yds. Kintyre Way walking trail. Whisky distilleries. Golf.

Open: April - end September.

Directions: Approaching from Glasgow (Erskine Bridge), take the A82 towards Crianlarich, past Loch Lomond. At Tarbet take the A83 towards Campbeltown, through Inveraray, Lochgilphead and Tarbert (Loch Fyne) and on to Muasdale Village, from where the site is well signed.

GPS: 55.597307, -5.686058

Charges guide

Per unit incl. 2 persons and electricity	£ 17.50 - £ 19.50
extra person	£ 2.00
child (5-15 yrs)	£ 1.25
dog	£ 1.25

Muasdale Holiday Park

Muasdale, Tarbert PA29 6XD (Argyll and Bute)
t: 01583 421207   e: enquiries@muasdaleholidays.com
alanrogers.com/UK7250   www.muasdaleholidays.com

Accommodation: ☑ Pitch ☑ Mobile home/chalet ○ Hotel/B&B ○ Apartment

Muasdale Holiday Park has a beach-side location with fine views of the sea and islands, between Campbeltown and Tarbert on Kintyre's west coast. This is a small, friendly site with just ten pitches for touring units, five for tents and one used for a caravan holiday home to rent. The pitches are situated on a level, grass field, all with unobstructed sea views. All have electrical connections. You are advised to anchor tents and awnings securely as the winds are sometimes strong and gusty. The beach is a magnificent expanse of white sand with rock pools and an abundance of wildlife. The sunsets are frequently breathtaking. Sea canoeing and sea fishing are both popular. The site prides itself on its 'get away from it all' nature. There are very few amenities here but there is a well stocked village shop just 100 m. away. There is no bar or restaurant. Barbecues are permitted on site, and campfires are also possible on the beach, provided that proper care is taken.

You might like to know

There are many rock pools to explore, and sea fishing and sea canoeing are popular.

- ☑ Beach on site
- ○ Beach within 1 km
- ☑ Sandy beach
- ○ Blue Flag quality
- ○ Lifeguard *(high season)*
- ○ Sun lounger and/or deckchair hire
- ☑ Watersports *(e.g. sailing or windsurfing)*
- ○ Snacks and drinks
- ○ Sunshades/sunbeds
- ○ Dogs allowed *(on the beach)*

Facilities: The toilet facilities can be heated. Showers have no divider or seat. Laundry. Motorcaravan services. The Anchorage restaurant at the entrance to the park (used as reception at quiet times) serves meals at reasonable prices, cooked to order (l/4-30/9). Boat launching. Fishing permits can be arranged. Off site: Village with shop and post office, gas is available from the petrol station and mobile banks visit regularly.

Open: Easter/1 April - 30 September, but phone first to check.

Directions: Park is by Scourie village on A894 road in northwest Sutherland.

GPS: 58.351417, -5.156767

Charges guide

Per unit incl. 2 persons
and electricity £ 24.40 - £ 29.40

No credit cards.

Scourie Caravan & Camping Park

Harbour Road, Scourie IV27 4TG (Highland)
t: 01971 502060
alanrogers.com/UK7730

Accommodation: ☑ Pitch ☑ Mobile home/chalet ○ Hotel/B&B ○ Apartment

Mr Mackenzie's family now run this park. There are a number of firm terraces with 60 pitches which gives it an attractive layout – there is nothing regimented here. Perched on the edge of the bay in an elevated position, practically everyone has a view of the sea and a short walk along the shore footpath leads to a small sandy beach. The park has tarmac and gravel access roads, with well drained grass and hardstanding pitches, some with 10A electric hook-ups. A few are on an area which is unfenced from the rocks (young children would need to be supervised here). Reception contains a wealth of tourist information and maps. There are very good facilities for disabled visitors on the park and at the restaurant, although the ramps leading to them are a little steep. Mr Mackenzie claims that this is the only caravan park in the world from where, depending on the season, you can see palm trees, Highland cattle and Great Northern divers from your pitch. Red throated divers have also been seen. Trips to Handa Island (a special protection area for seabird colonies) are available from here and Tarbet. The clear water makes this area ideal for diving.

You might like to know

The small sandy beach is a short walk from the site. It has crystal clear water and is great for swimming and fishing from the rocks. There is also a bird hide.

○ Beach on site
☑ Beach within 1 km
☑ Sandy beach
○ Blue Flag quality
○ Lifeguard *(high season)*
○ Sun lounger and/or deckchair hire
○ Watersports *(e.g. sailing or windsurfing)*
○ Snacks and drinks
○ Sunshades/sunbeds
○ Dogs allowed *(on the beach)*

Been to any good campsites lately?
We have

You'll find them here...

... also here...

101 great campsites, ideal for your specific hobby,
pastime or passion

Want independent campsite reviews at your fingertips?

You'll find them here...

Over 3,000 in-depth campsite reviews at
www.alanrogers.com

...and even here...

Want to book your holiday on one of Europe's top campsites?

We can do it for you. No problem.

The best campsites in the most popular regions - we'll take care of everything

alan rogers travel

alan rogers

Discover the best campsites in Europe
with Alan Rogers

alanrogers.com
01580 214000

Index

Index

Index